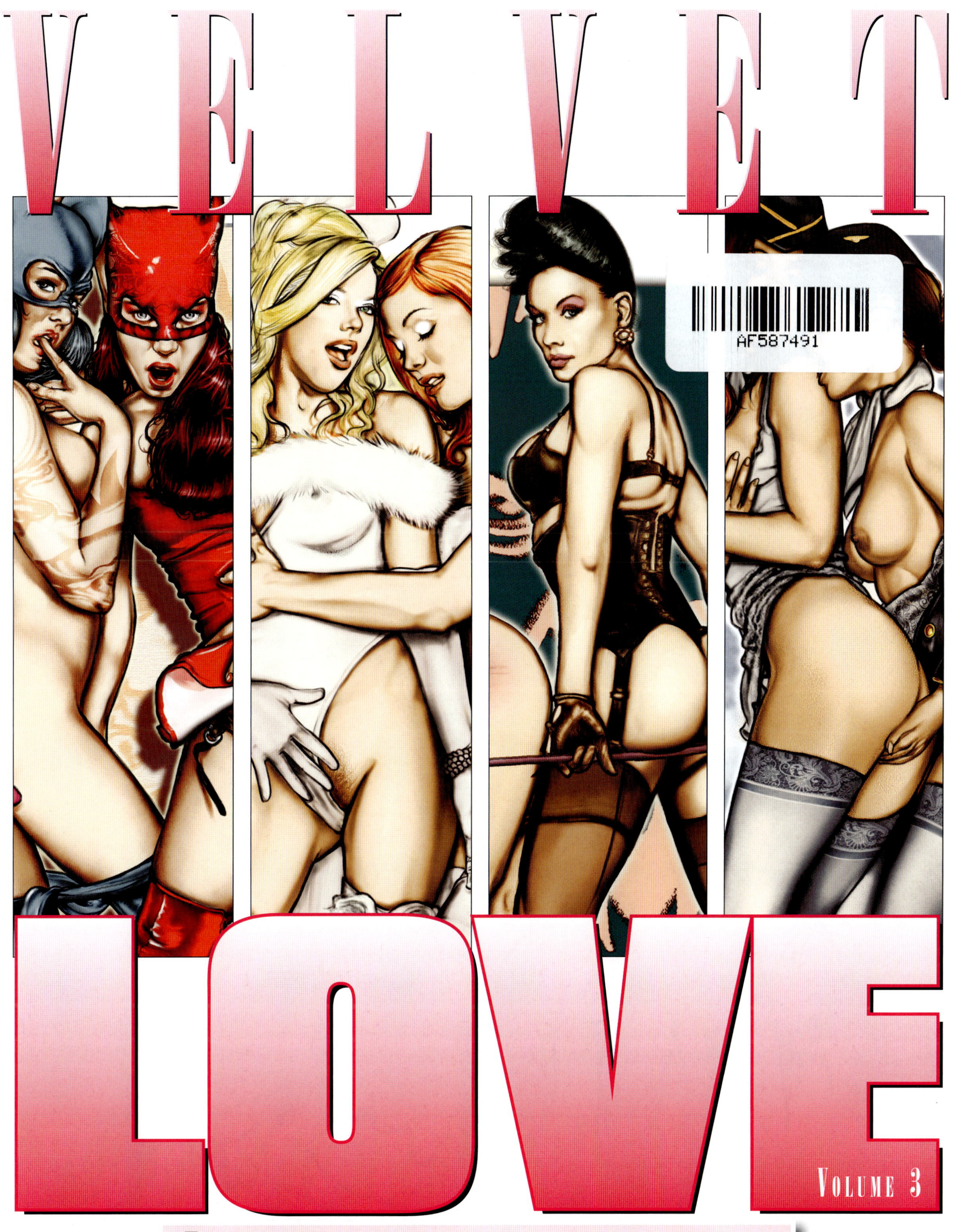

VELVET LOVE

Volume 3

The glory of girl on girl on girl by

Mazzotti & Andrei

AN SQP PRESENTATION

A, B and C: The Game of Language

The game is simple. Licking each other between her thighs.
A licks B and C. B then A and then licks C. C licks A, then B...
then invert the order. A then B. B and C licks C.
A licks C, then B, then A.. .
And the taste on their tongues are mixed into a single essence.

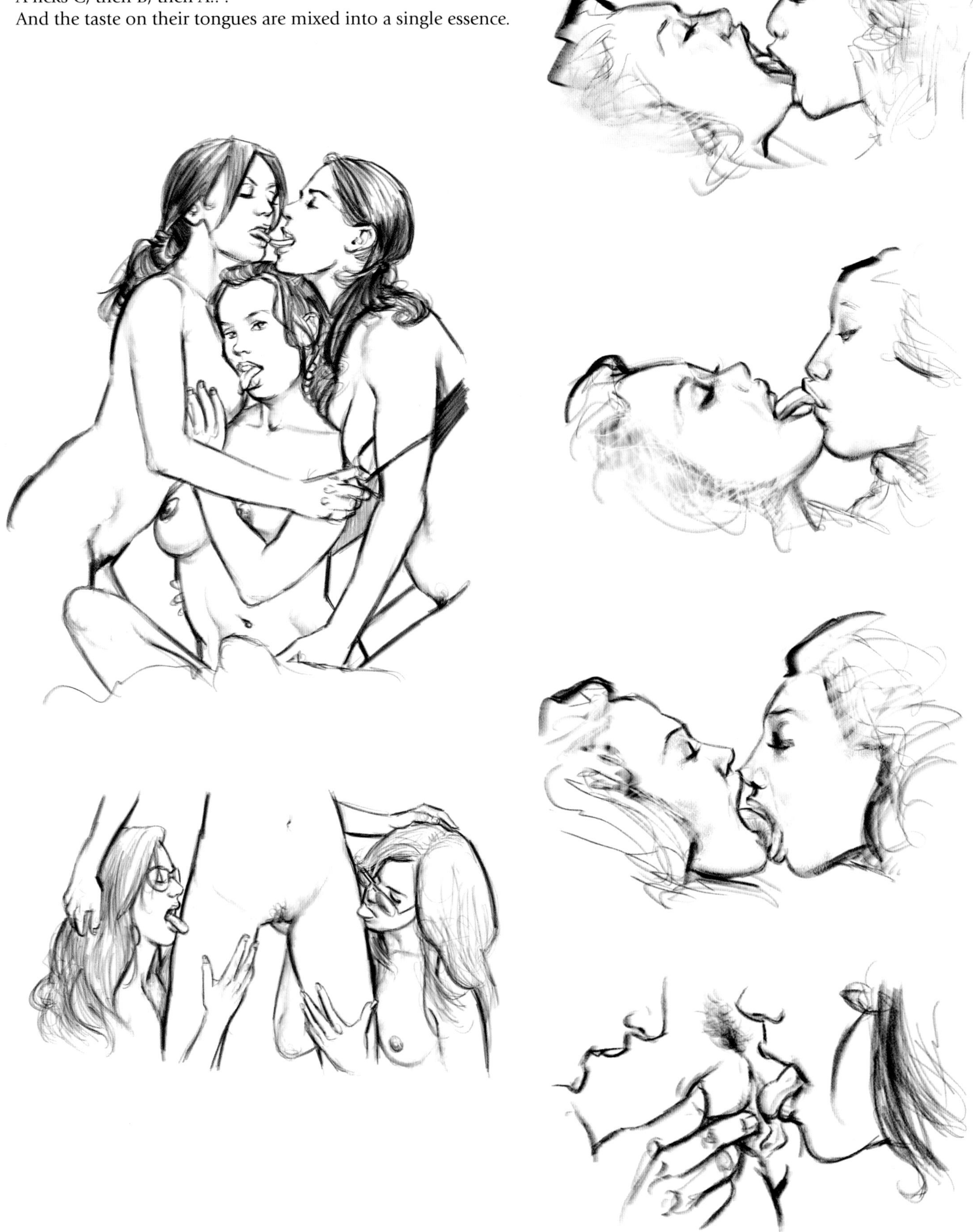

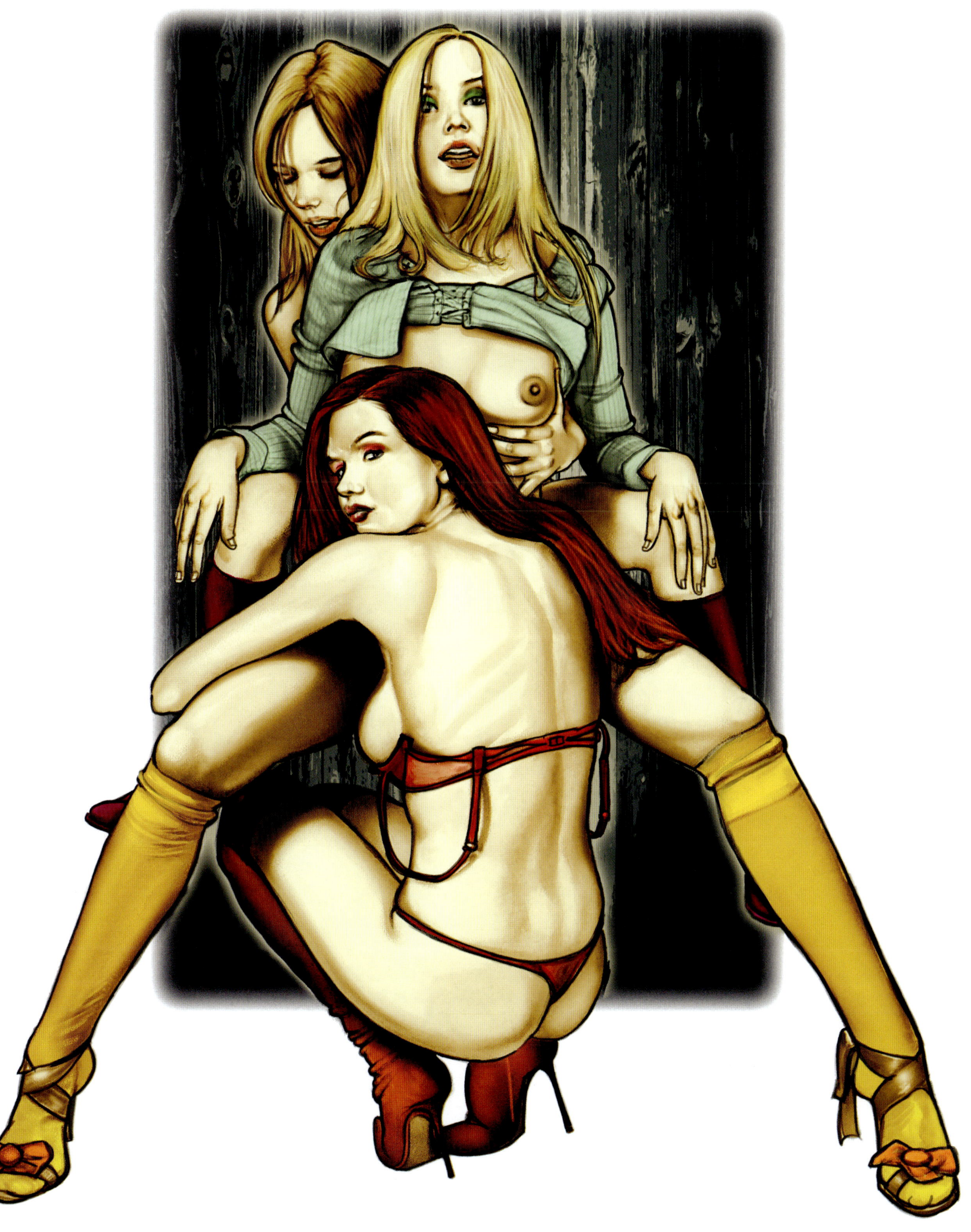

Any Given Sunday

Are rooting for the local team: muscular handsome males ... certainly interesting. But during the game play too. They prefer to burrow into the locker room and play hard, licking with a repetition and reciprocal actions in the game.
Up to orgasm: touchdown!
Kick off ...

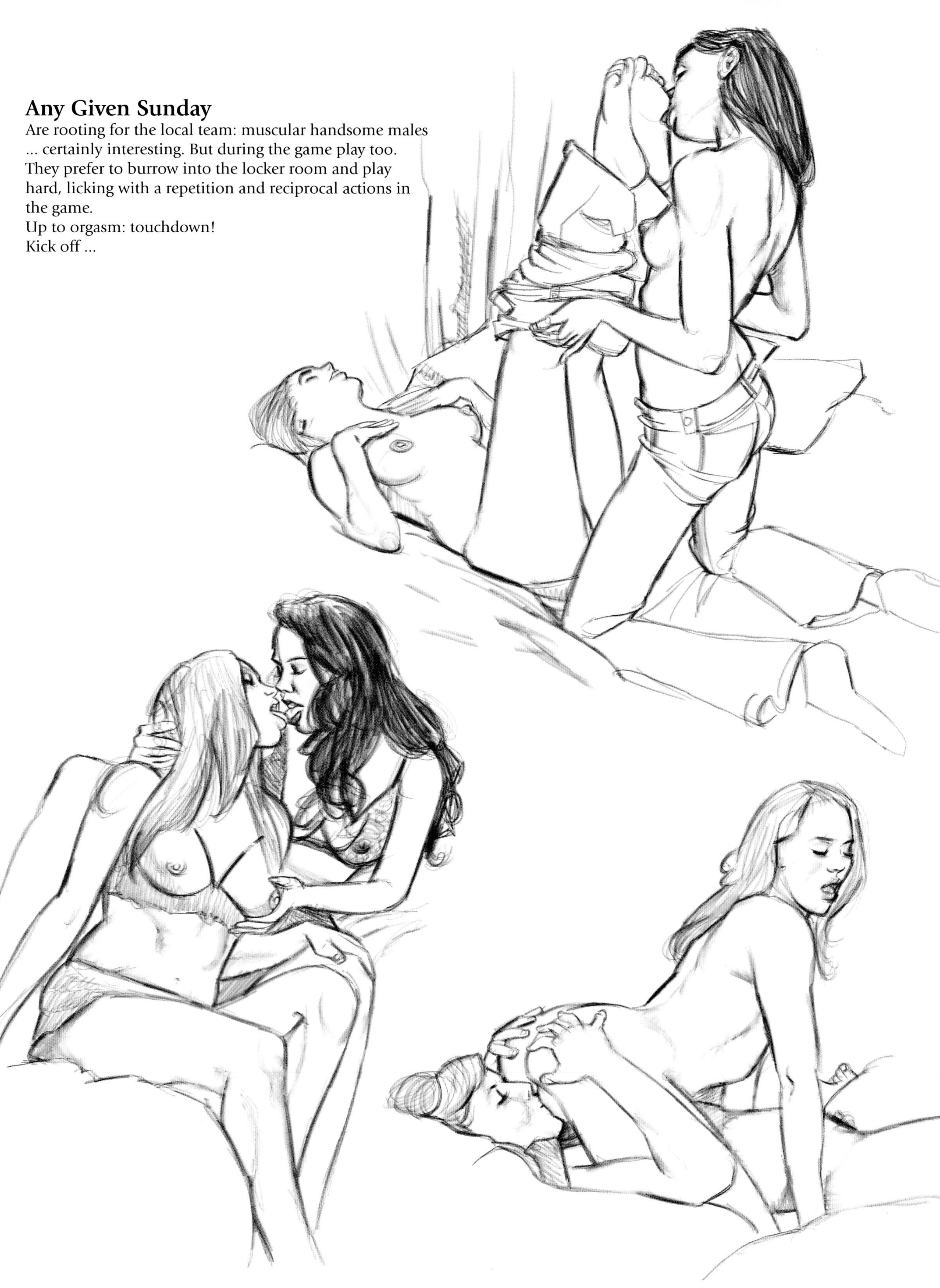

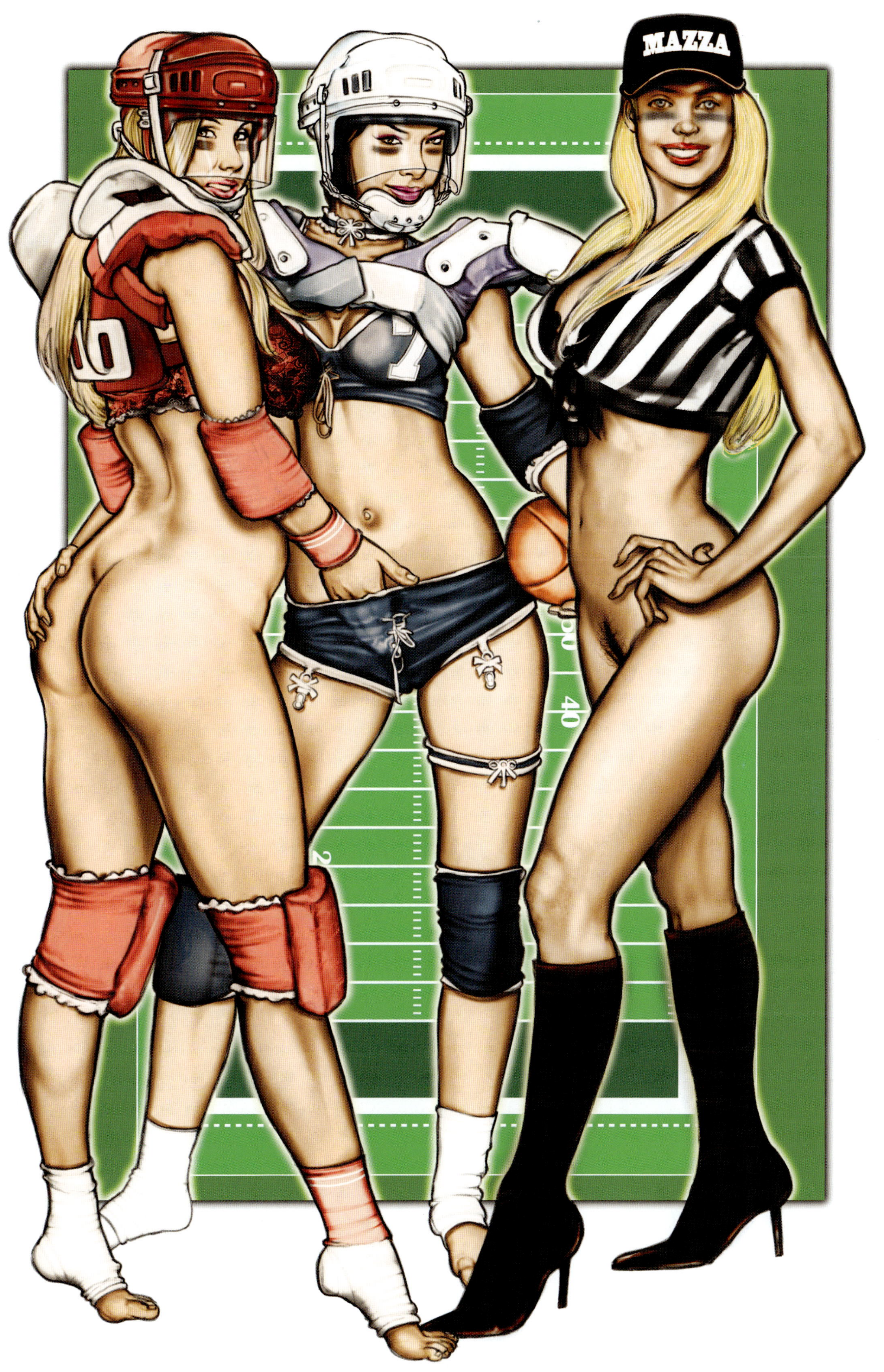
MAZZA
7
40

Cosplayer

Fans love to dress up as heroes from their favorite pop culture comics and films, hunting for alien monsters, or imagining scenes from a demonic dimension. As they grow older, the costumes begin to mutate, giving shape to new characters and desires. They enter into hybrid territories of erotic passions. The magic wands of white fairies transform into strap-on dildos lubricated to stun the monsters deep into their deepest hell.

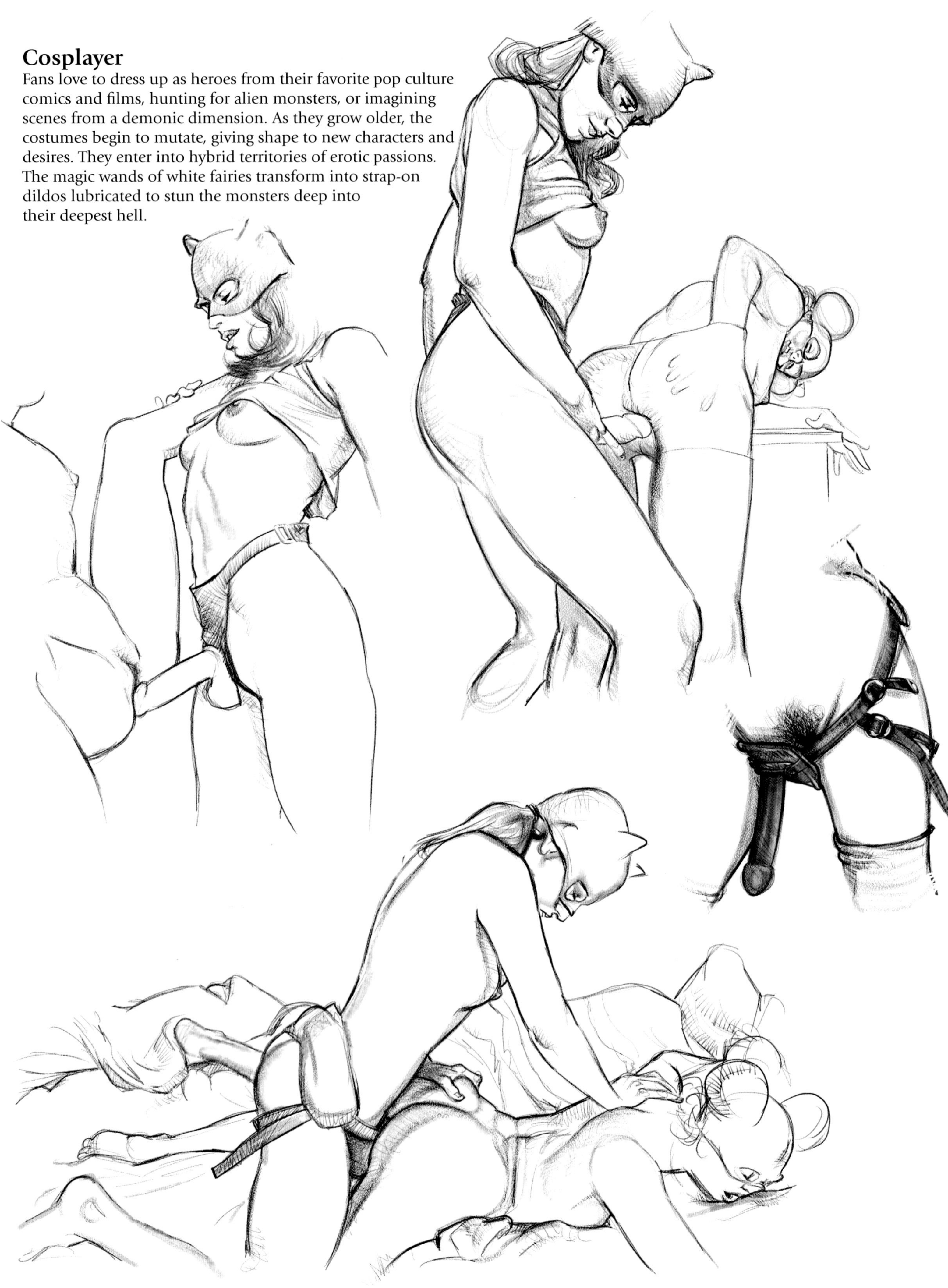

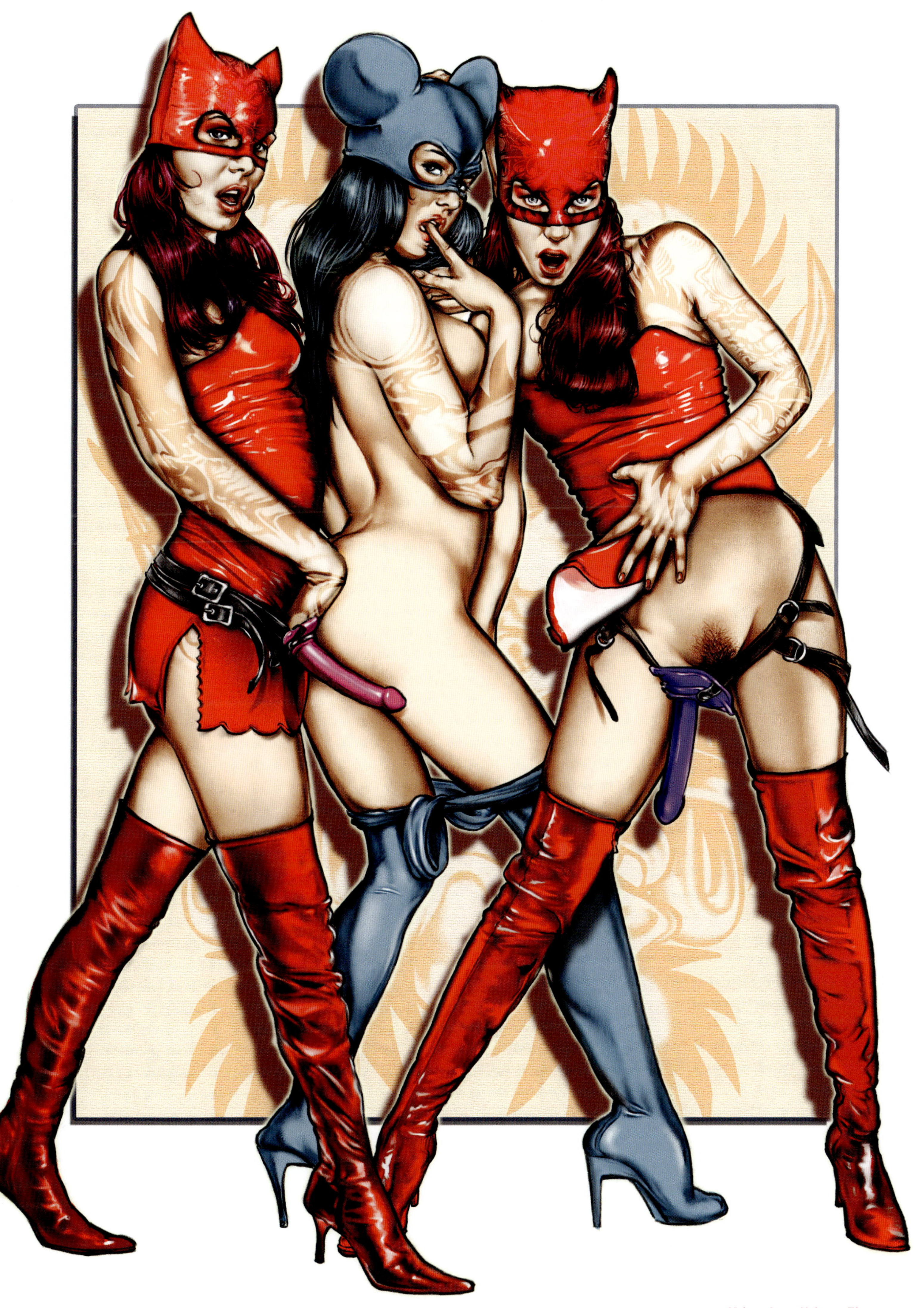

House Keeping

It was a hotel in desperate need of an overhaul. Yes, it had old world charm and had survived both world wars, but the plumbing was dreadful and the electricity was positively Edison-era. That said, the service in this French establishment more than made up for these shortcomings in the maid service. Simply pick up the phone (oh look - still rotary!) and dial "3". Before you know it, needs you didn't even know you had are being serviced. And well!

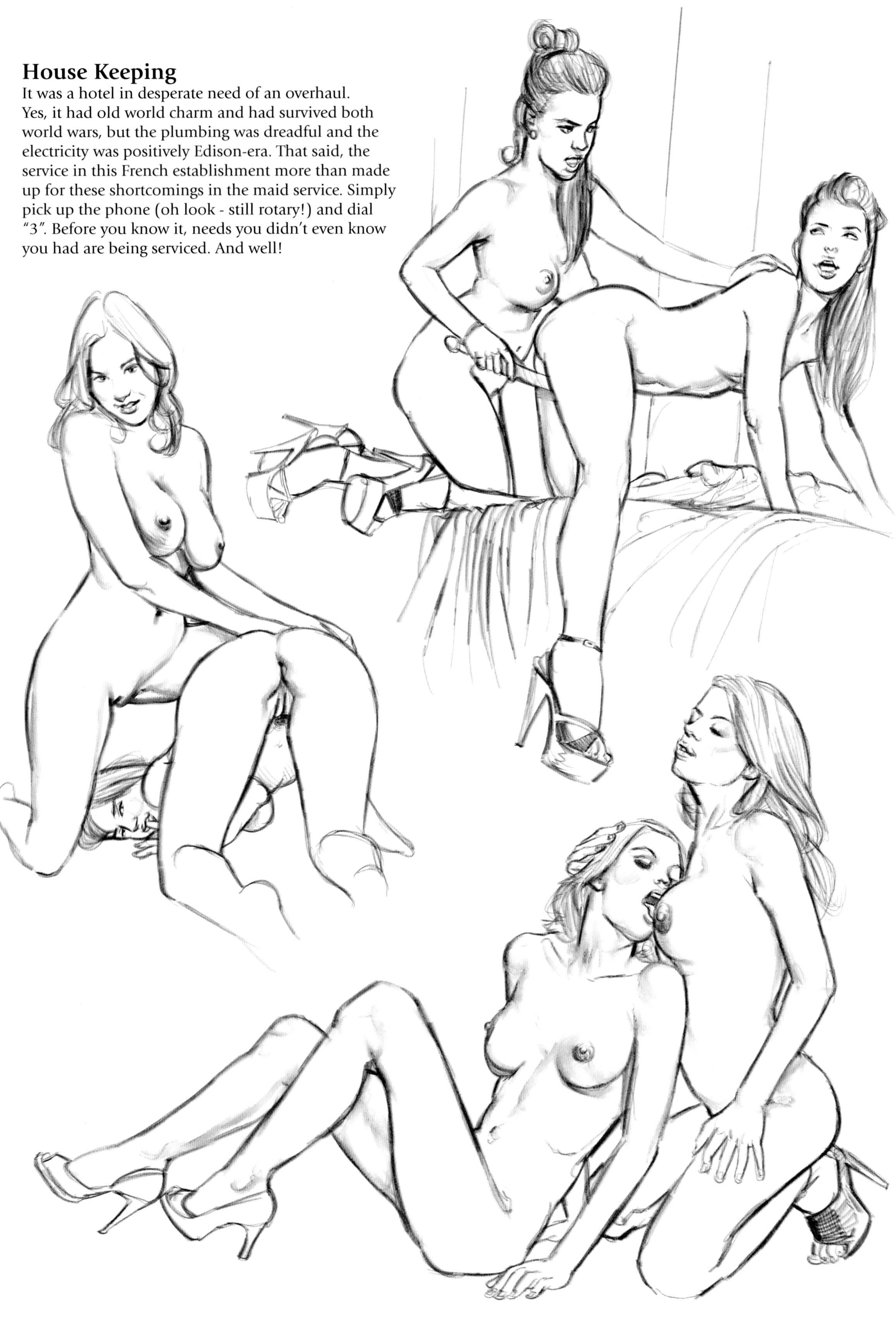

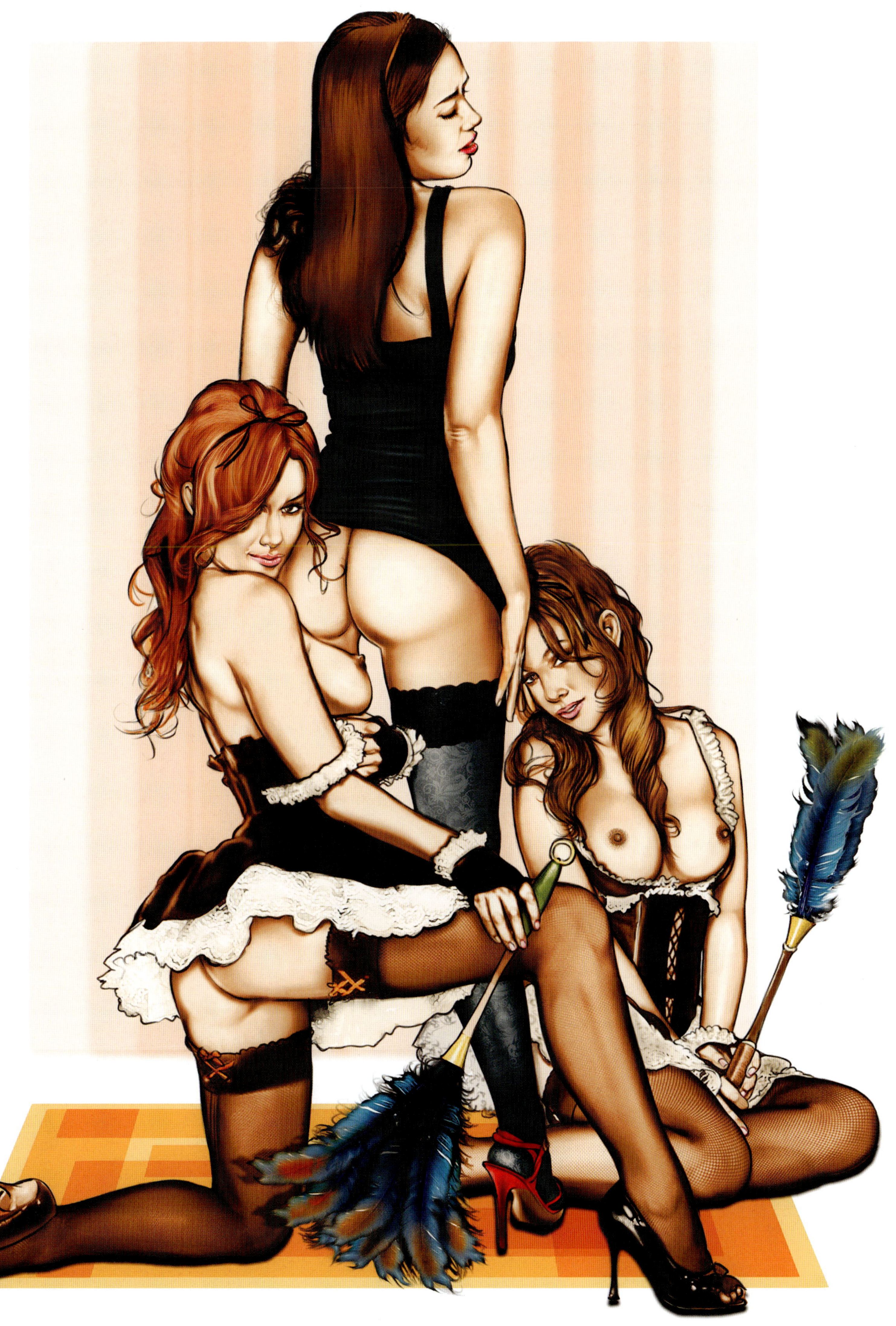

Dominatrix

Two slaves. Fleshy, tightly fastened to restraints.
She, the mistress, with corsets and stockings,
long gloves and flogger, paddle, whip, leash ...
... tools to make the flesh of slaves streaked with
purple, pain, suffering ...
Humiliated and submissive.

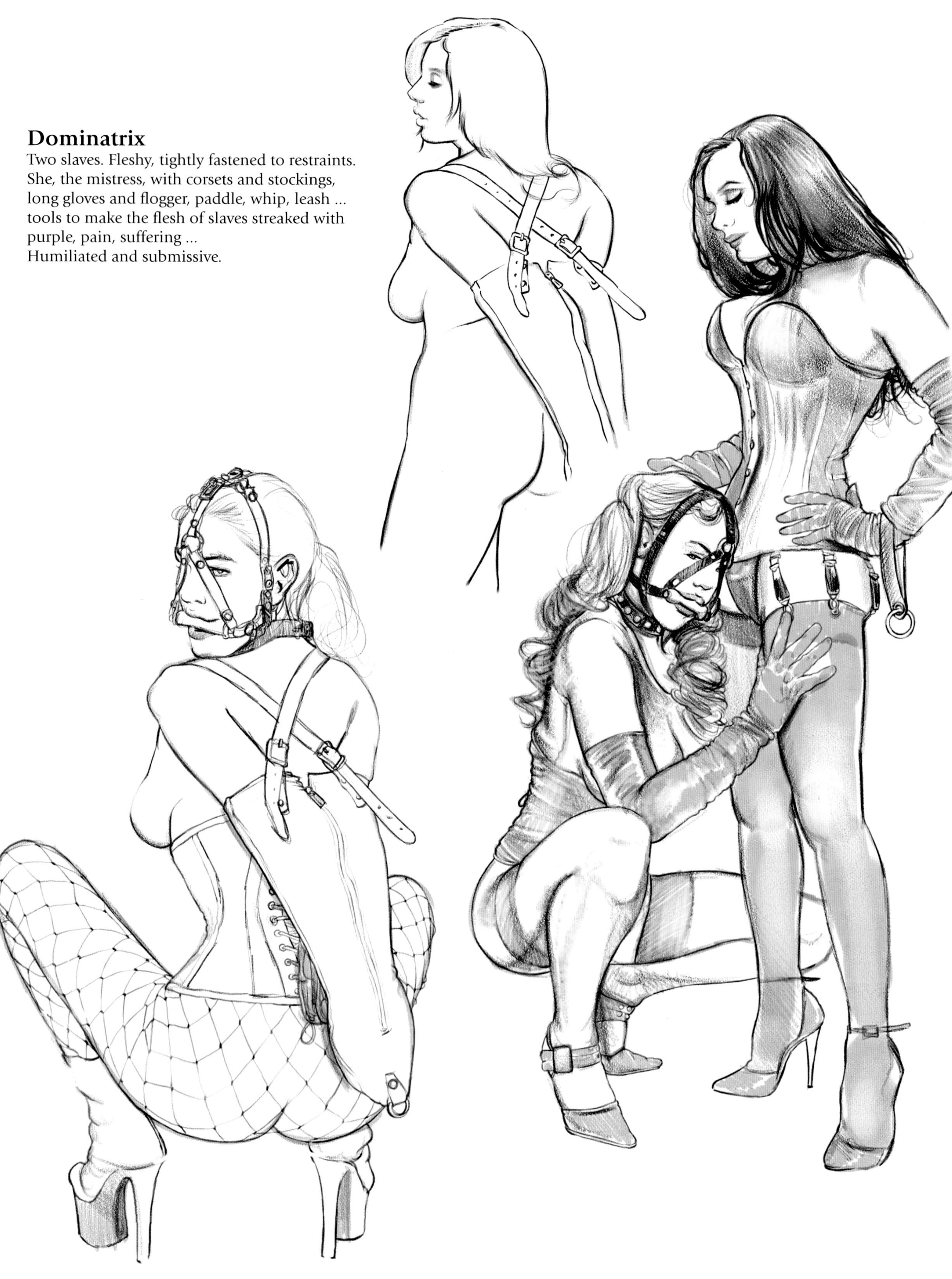

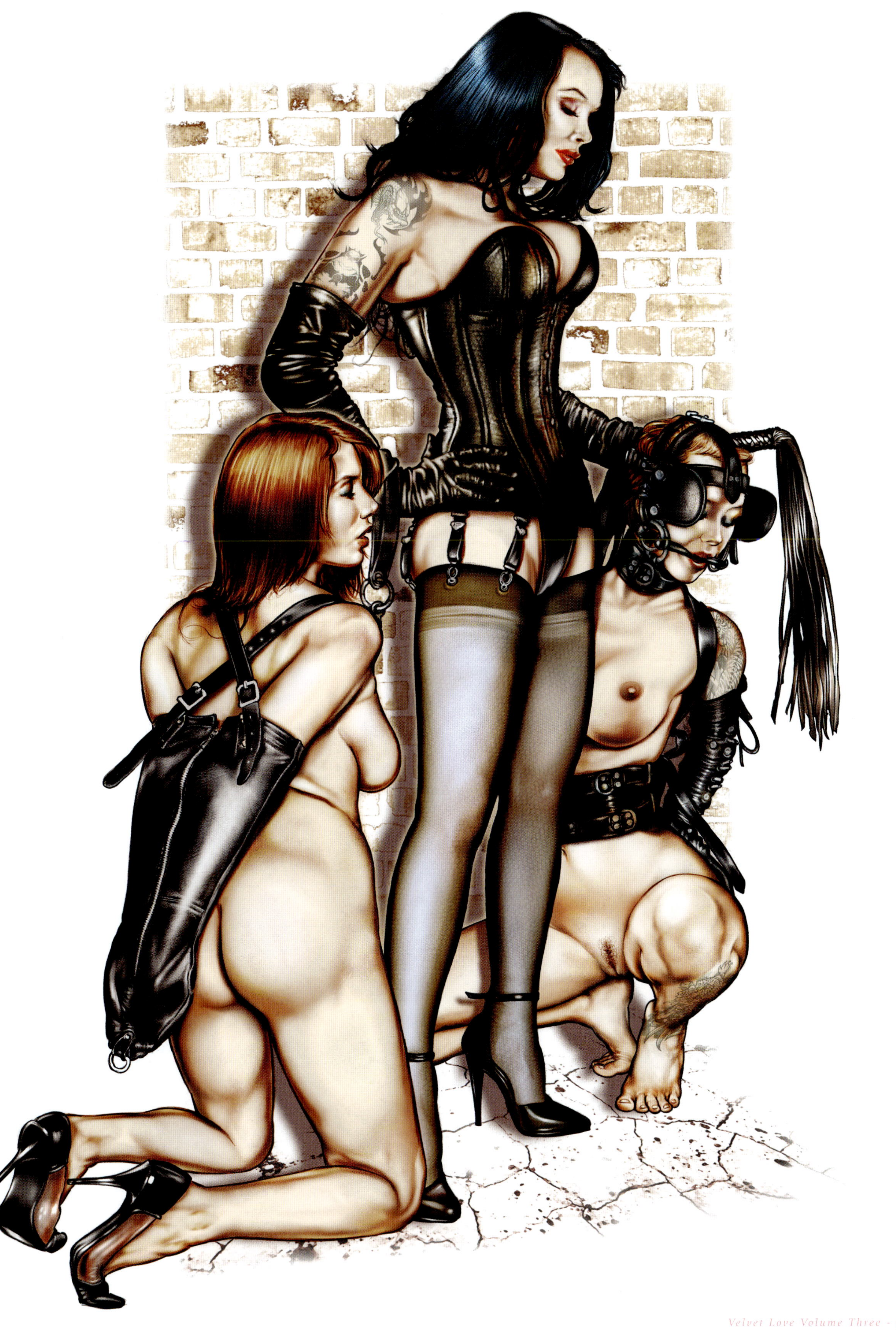

Honey

Three sweets in the dorm room that smells of baby powder and pizza boxes, scattered with textbooks and stuffed toys and discarded underwear. They're cramming for an exam but the hour is late, and giddiness is quickly turning into something else. A late-night snack has blossomed into something of a teaching aid. That jar of organic honey brings glorious wisdom, smeared and licked and spread, especially in the crevices. There ***will*** be a test...

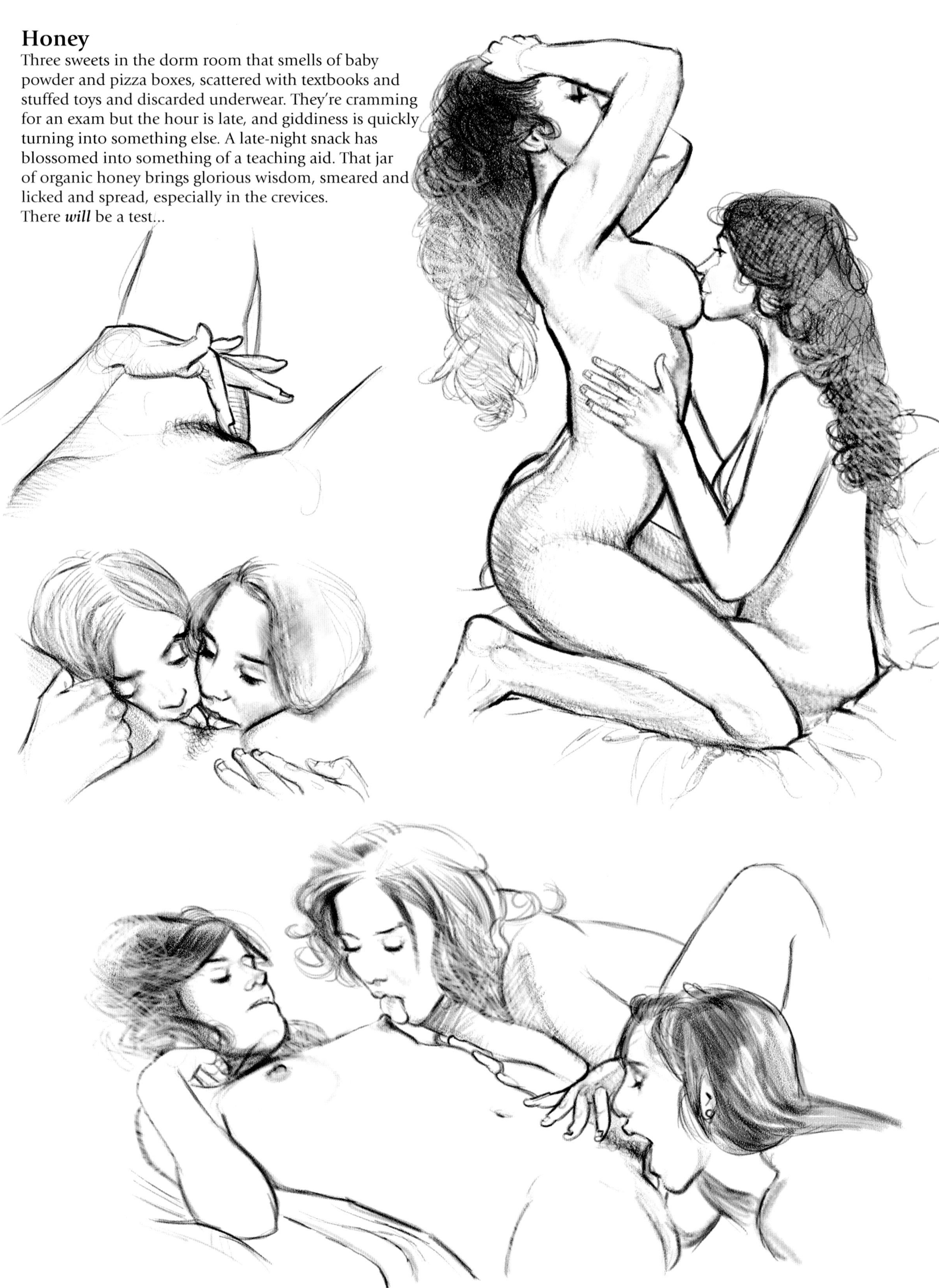

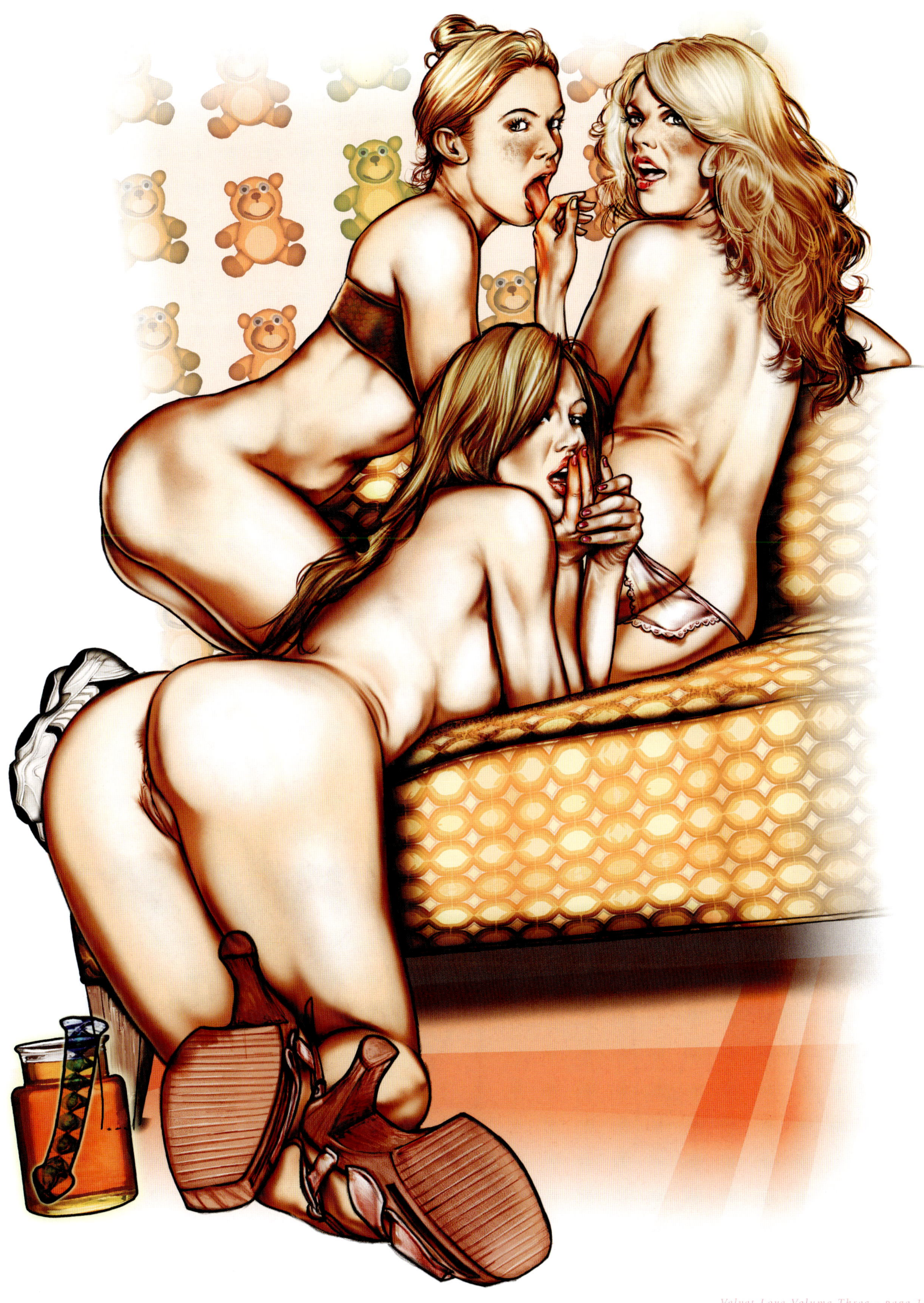

The Calendar

They run a downtown boutique, know nothing about sports, but they know a good opportunity when it comes banging on their door! In a professional photo studio, they strip down and dress up for a promotional calendar, sponsored by the local sports bar. They're pretty sure the combination of sports, alcohol, and ladies lingerie will help all three business for the next 365 days. Becoming neighborhood sex symbols should also help make working at the shop even more interesting than usual!

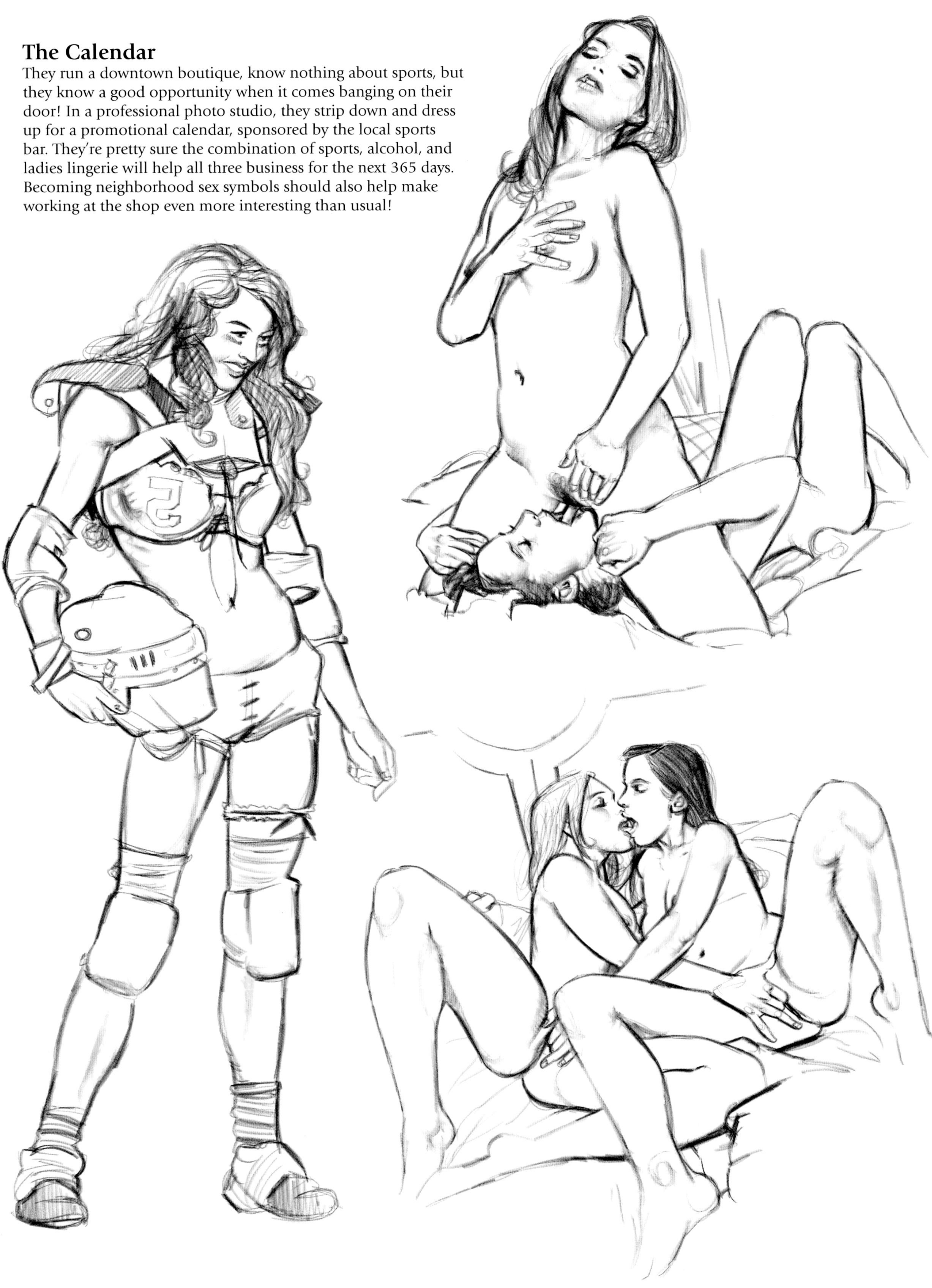

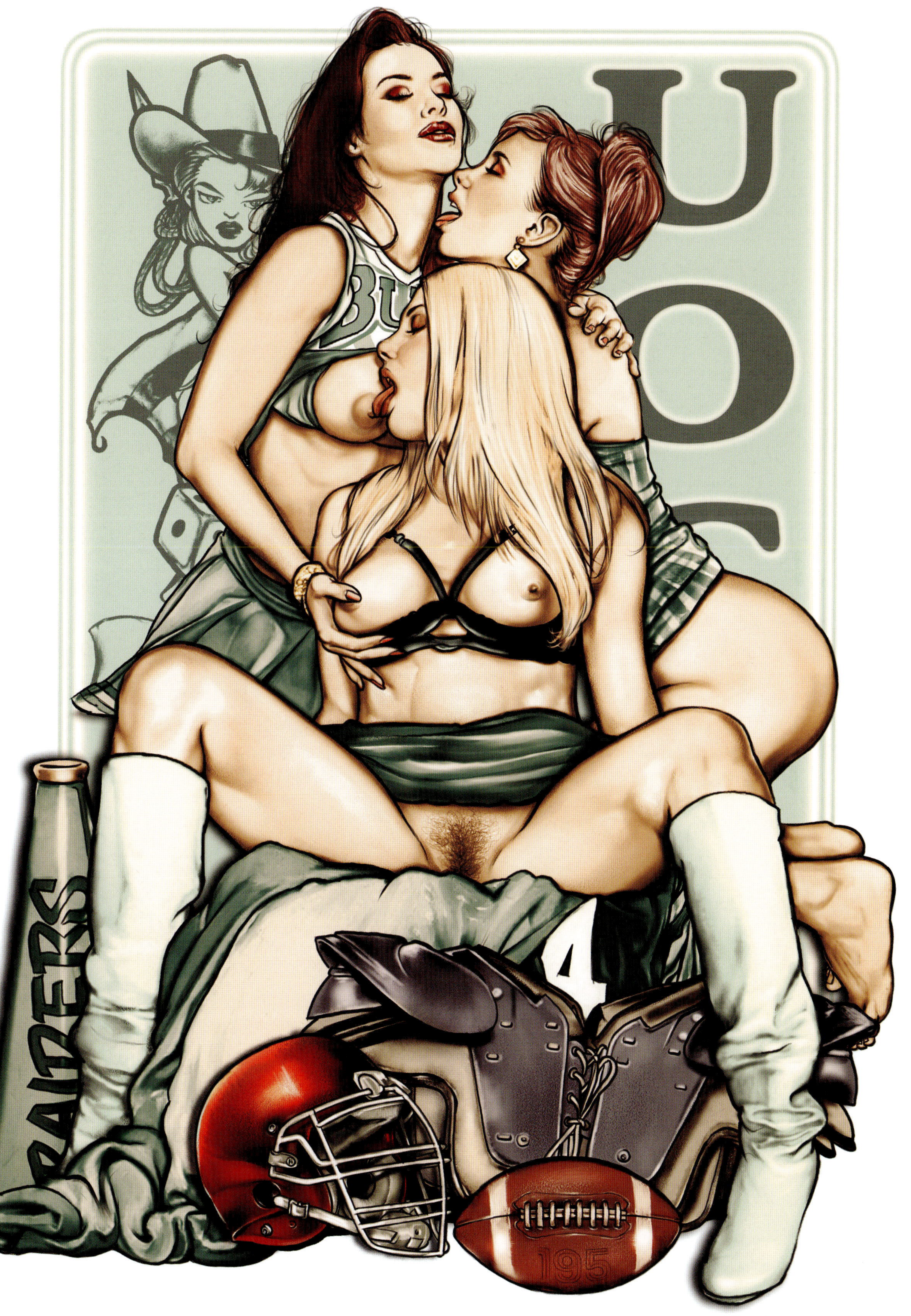
RAIDERS
195

The Wedding Day

Their best friend is getting married today.
The dressing of the bride, an intimate moment, second only to the central rite of the bed.
The bridesmaids honor their gentle duty with knowing hands and warm embraces lost in white lingerie and veils of tulle. The girls take loving care of every detail, to soothe their friend so very tense on this most important day.

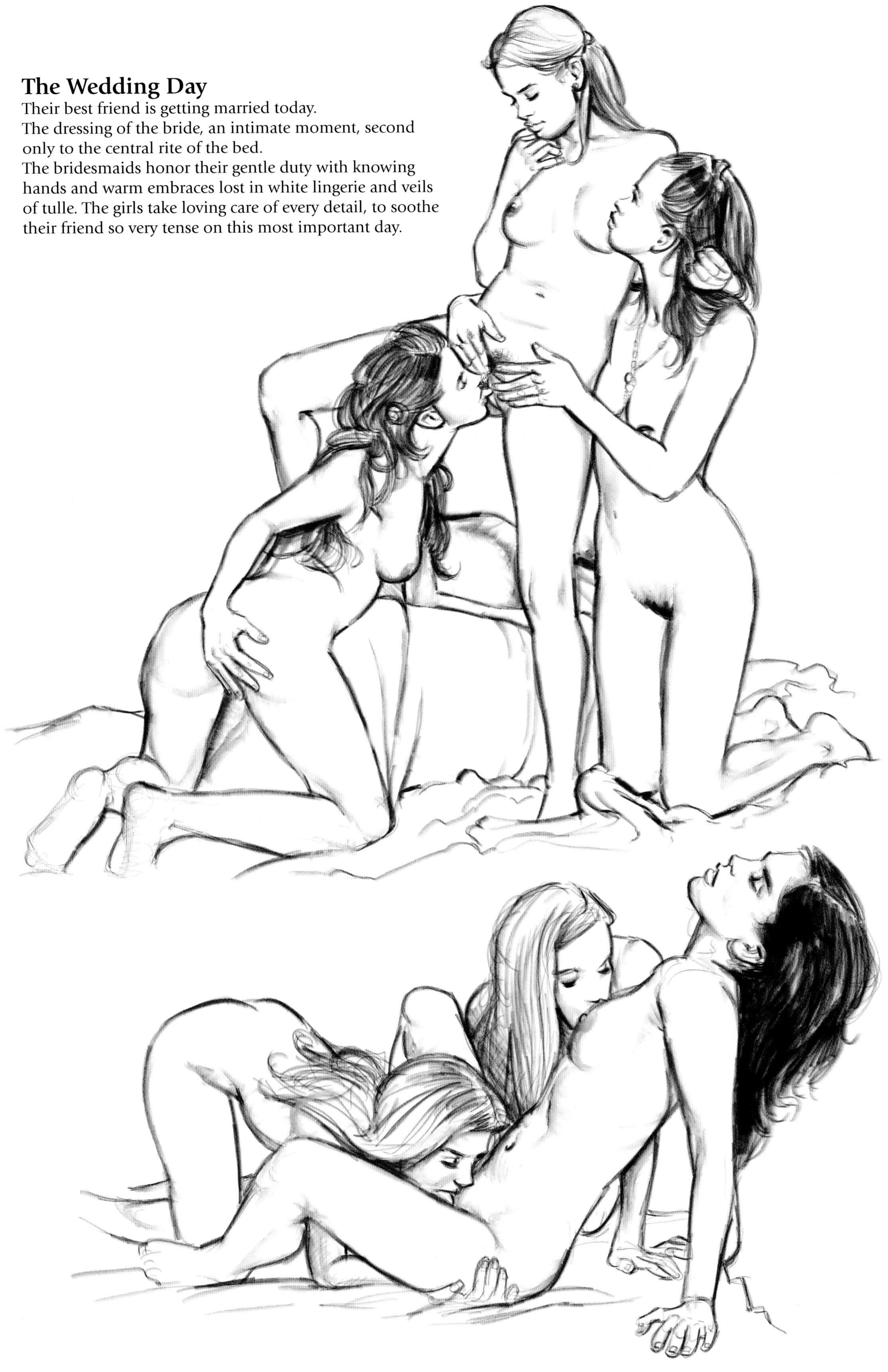

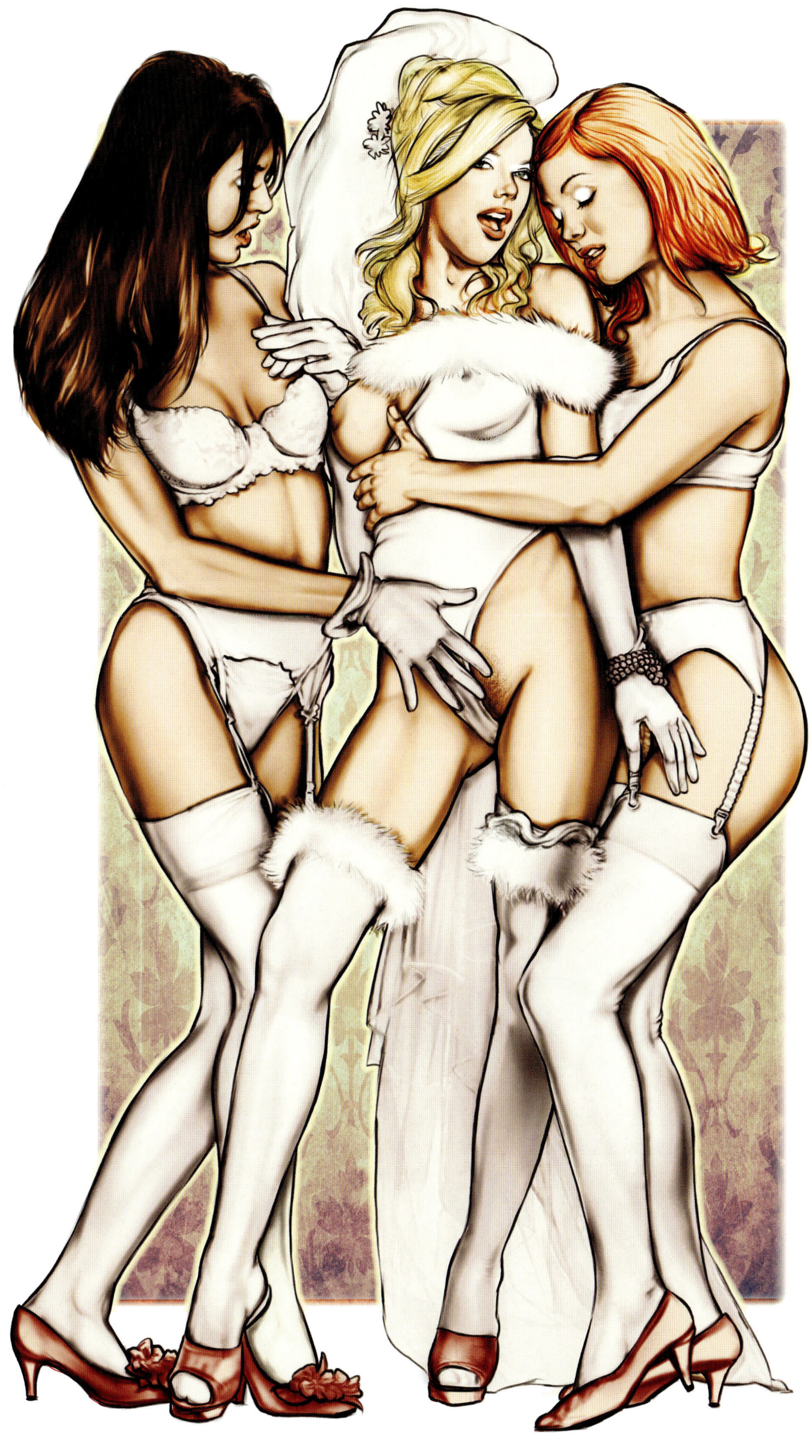

The Rodeo

The Annual Wild West State Fair always includes bull riding and bronco-busting, with plenty of cowboys and tests of skill. Sharpshooting, lasso-tossing, cow-roping - all big hits with the fans. That's the outdoor show.

The indoor show? The one the public doesn't see? That's where the cowgirls excel at their particular skills! You're gonna need a special pass to get to see *this* part of the rodeo, but once in, you're in for the show of a lifetime! Yippy-ki-yay, indeed! Giddy-up little ladies!

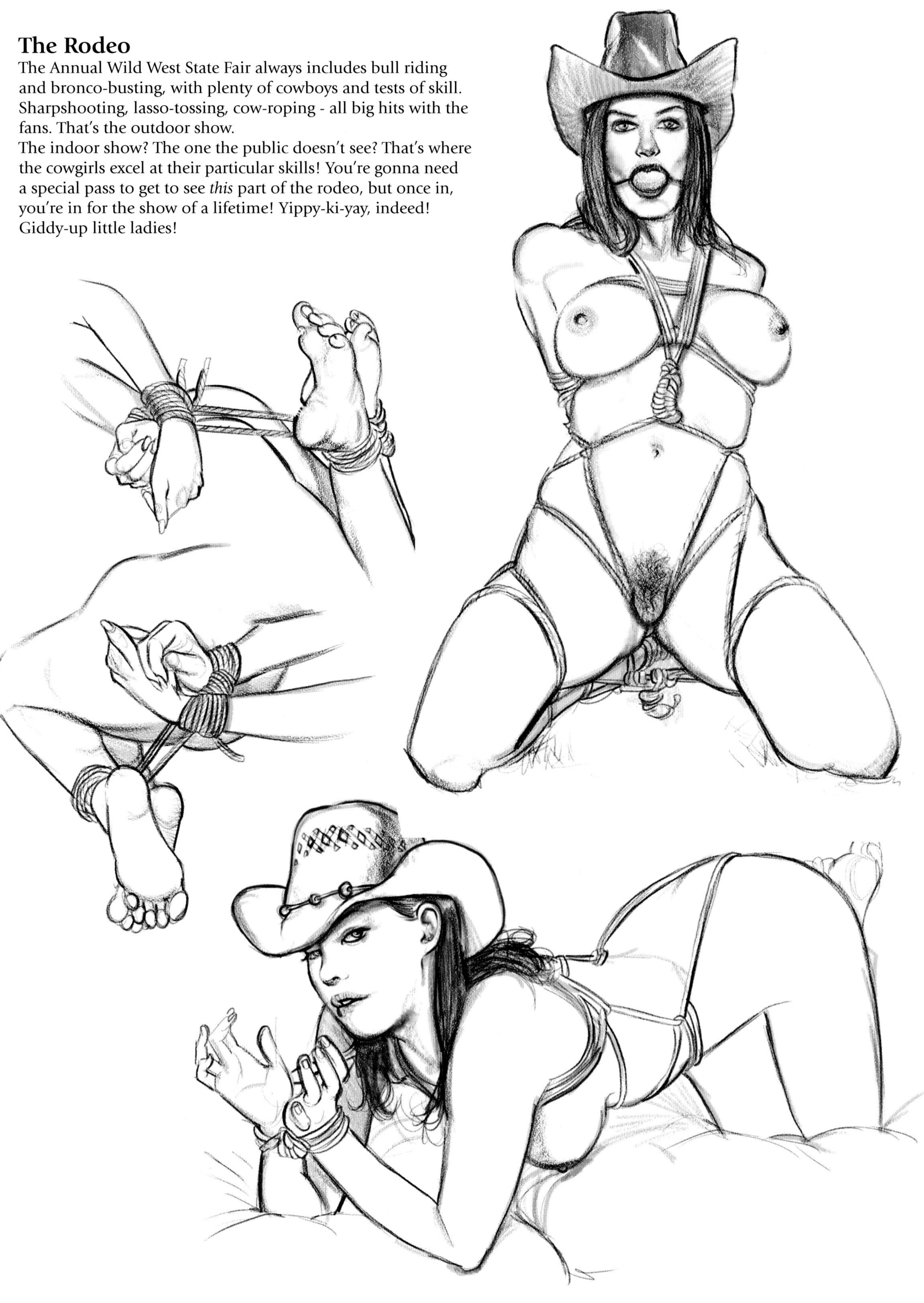

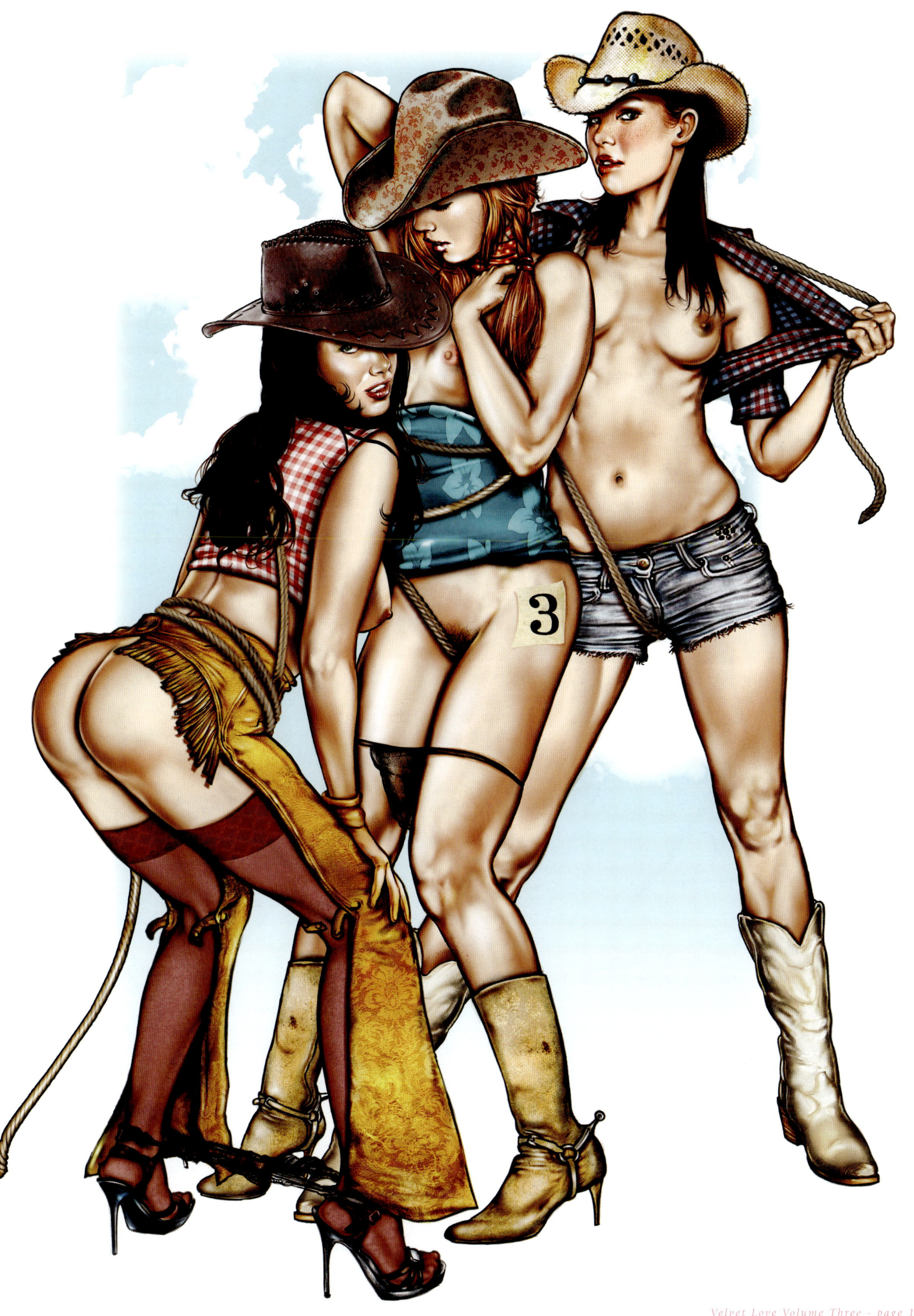
3

In Flight

I'm a flight attendant for intercontinental flights. Long red-eye transpacific flights that keep the cabin dark and quiet and filled with sleeping passengers. In first class, not everyone is always asleep. On the route to Tokyo, there are always a few well-heeled voyeurs who pay an extra fee for some extra service. A little show my friends and I usually perform for ourselves, but we're not against a little mile-high entertainment. Seats and tray-tables aren't the *only* thing that are in an upright position!

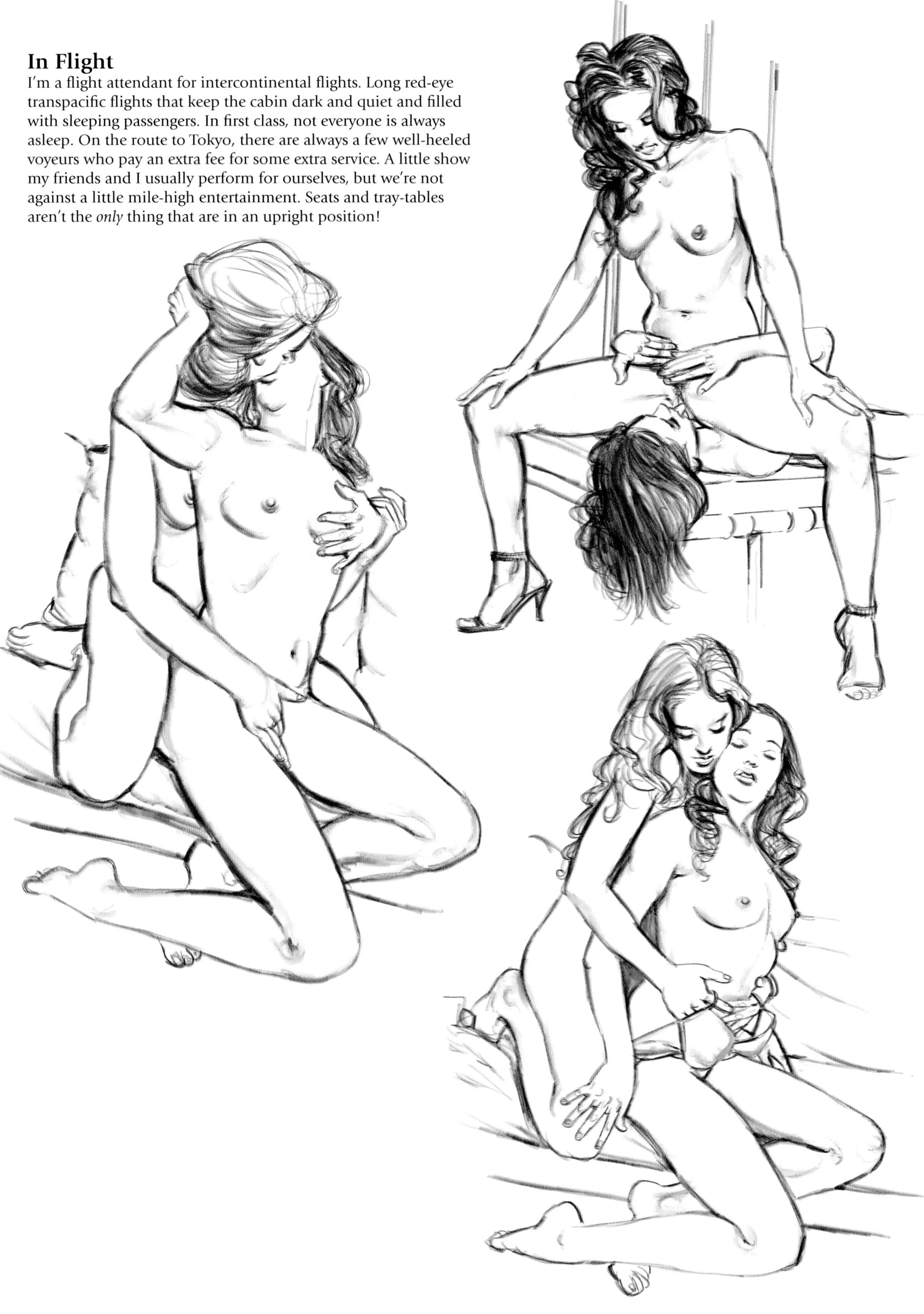

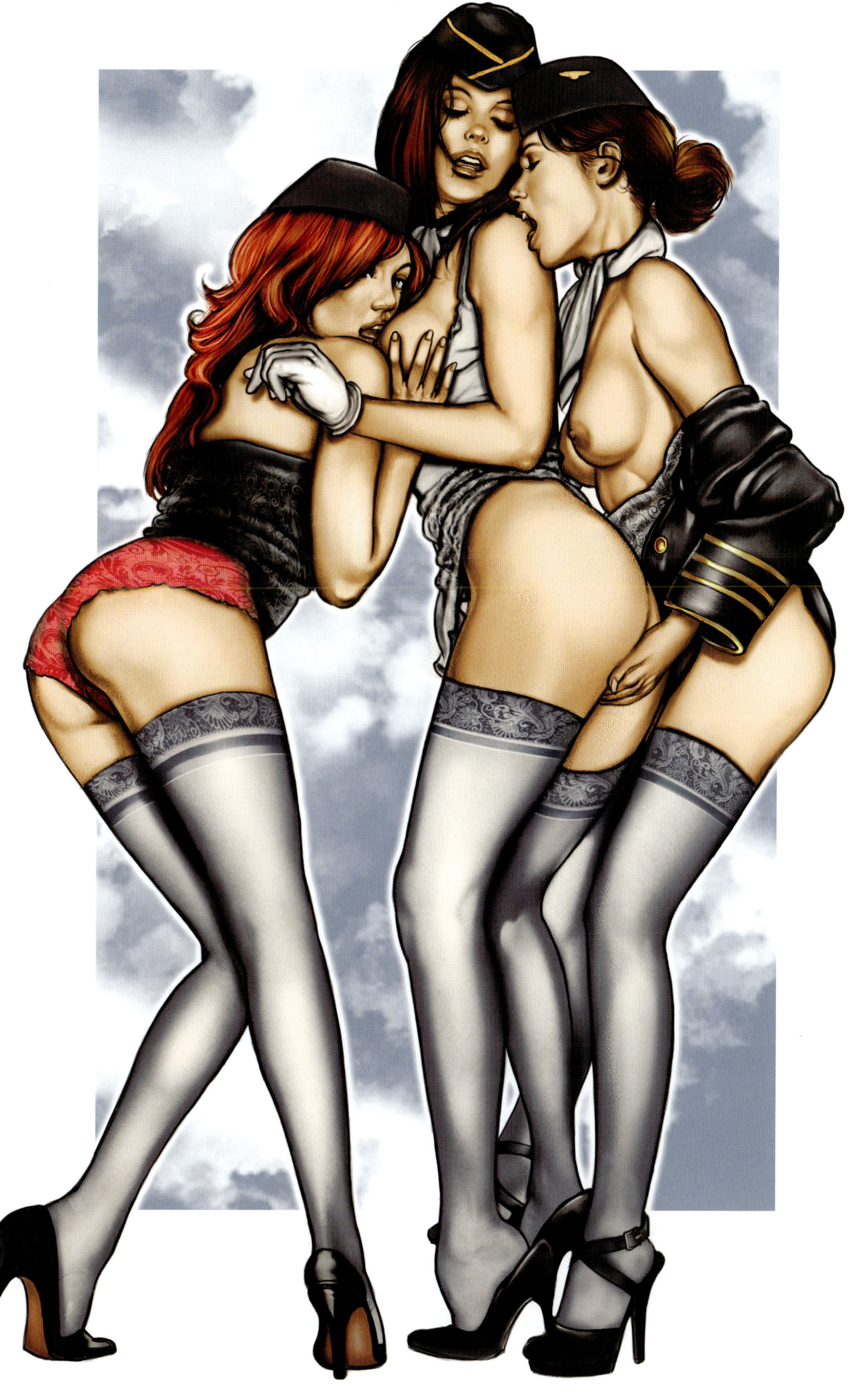

Nurse

Nursing is a noble profession.
These three student nurses are learning by hands-on training the intricacies of the human body. The female human body. The horny, writhing, aching to climax female human body.
Nothing beats *"learning by doing"*!

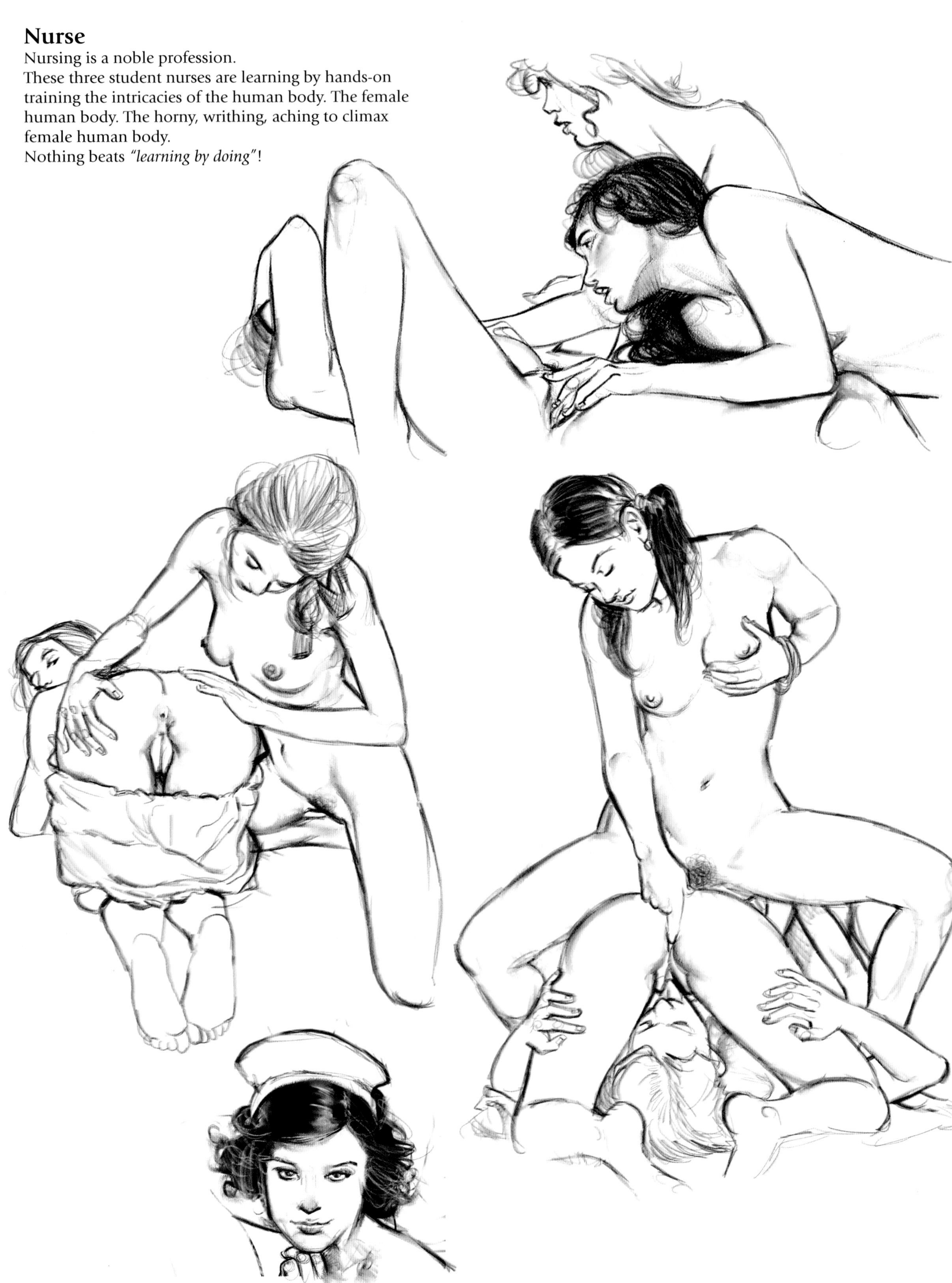

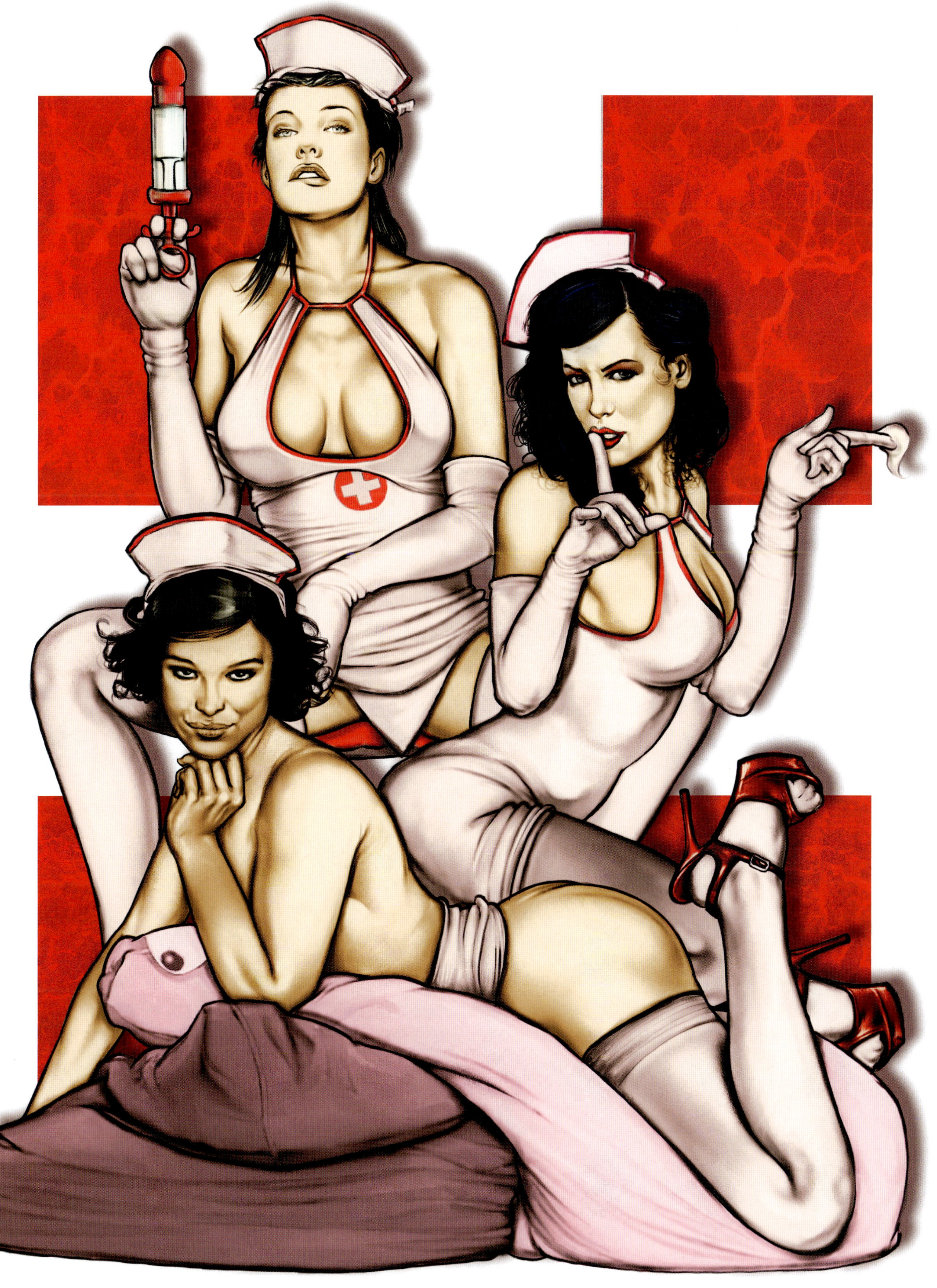

Famous For Being Famous

They wanted to feel the warm embrace of celebrity, and didn't really care what they had to do to get it. What could three girls and a website do to attract enough attention? Oh, that's right - the internet!

Installing a few web-cams and giving their IT guy plenty of snacks, soda, and hand-jobs was easy enough. Coming up with new ways to shock and awe - *that* was the challenge! Twelve days and 25,000,000 hits later, it seems these young ladies are poised for stardom. Hopefully it'll last another twelve days!

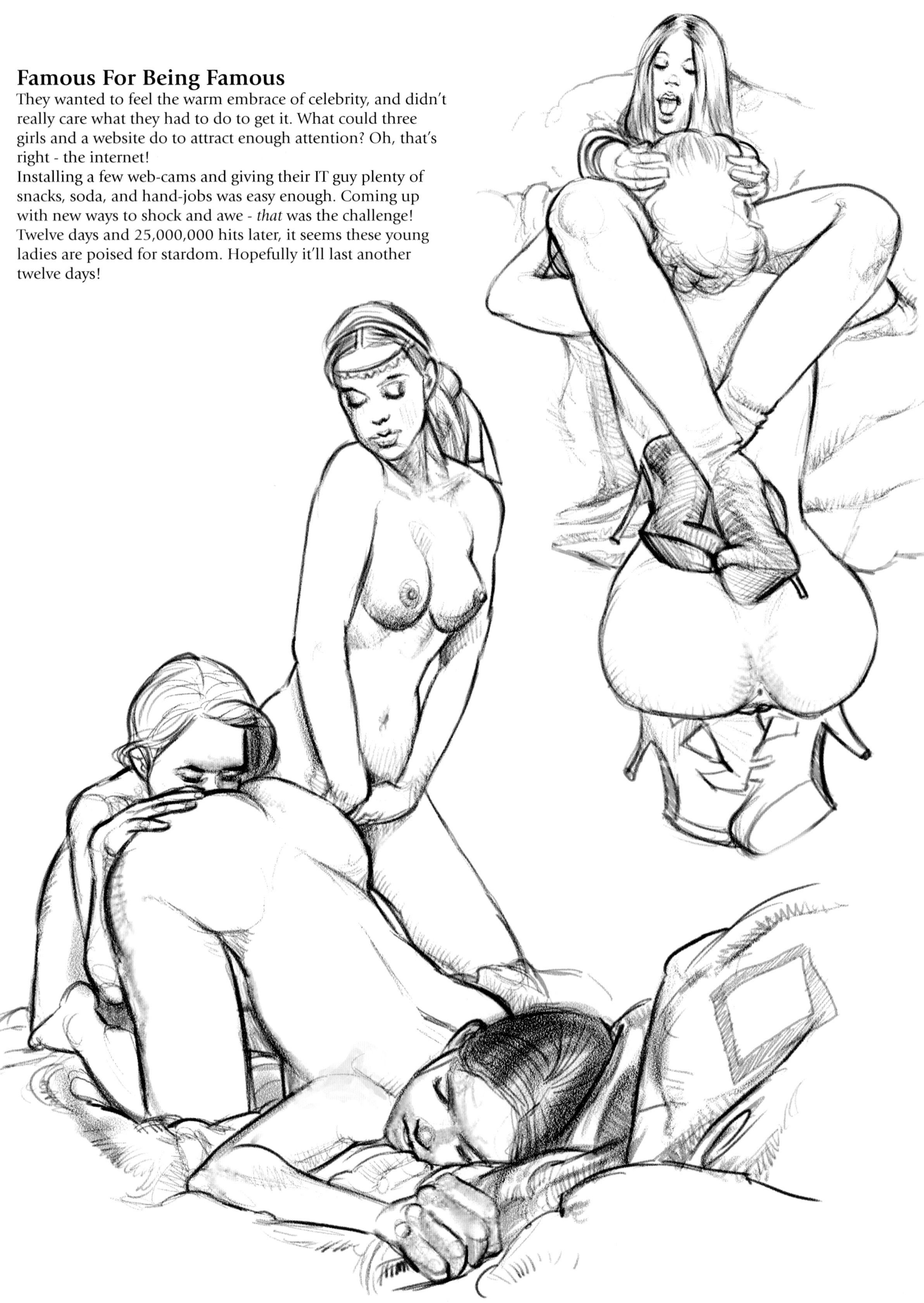

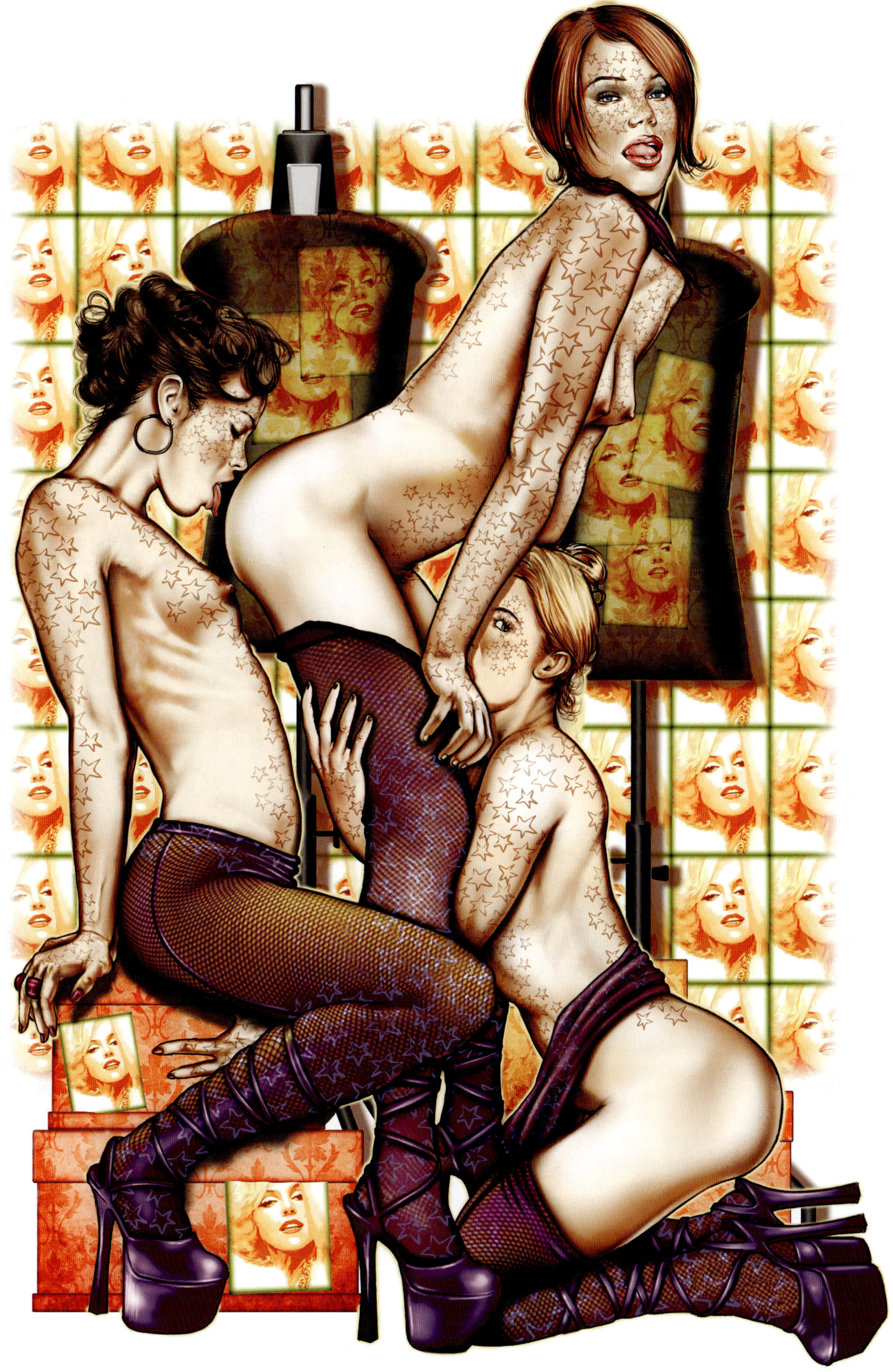

The Prisoner

Three hours of captivity. Three long hours ... the accused has a long record of offenses, both petty and profane. The profane is what's being dealt with right now in a special room they call *"The Box"*. In here, the time-tested method of "good cop - bad cop" has been replaced with "hot cop - horny cop". The phallic clubs and handcuffs are standard issue, and the information they're going to get out of this prisoner will come in the form of moans and screams. Good thing the box is sound-proof!

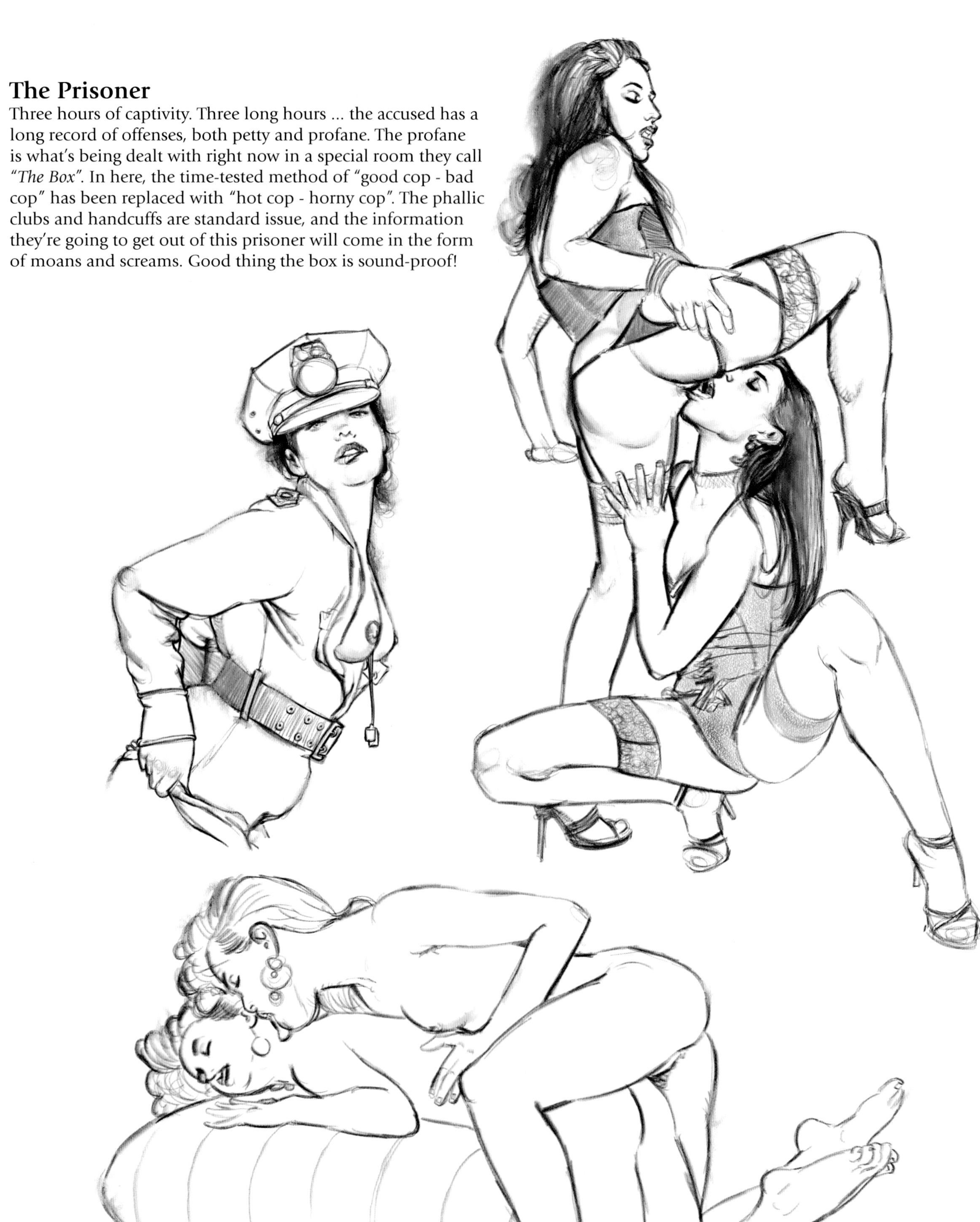

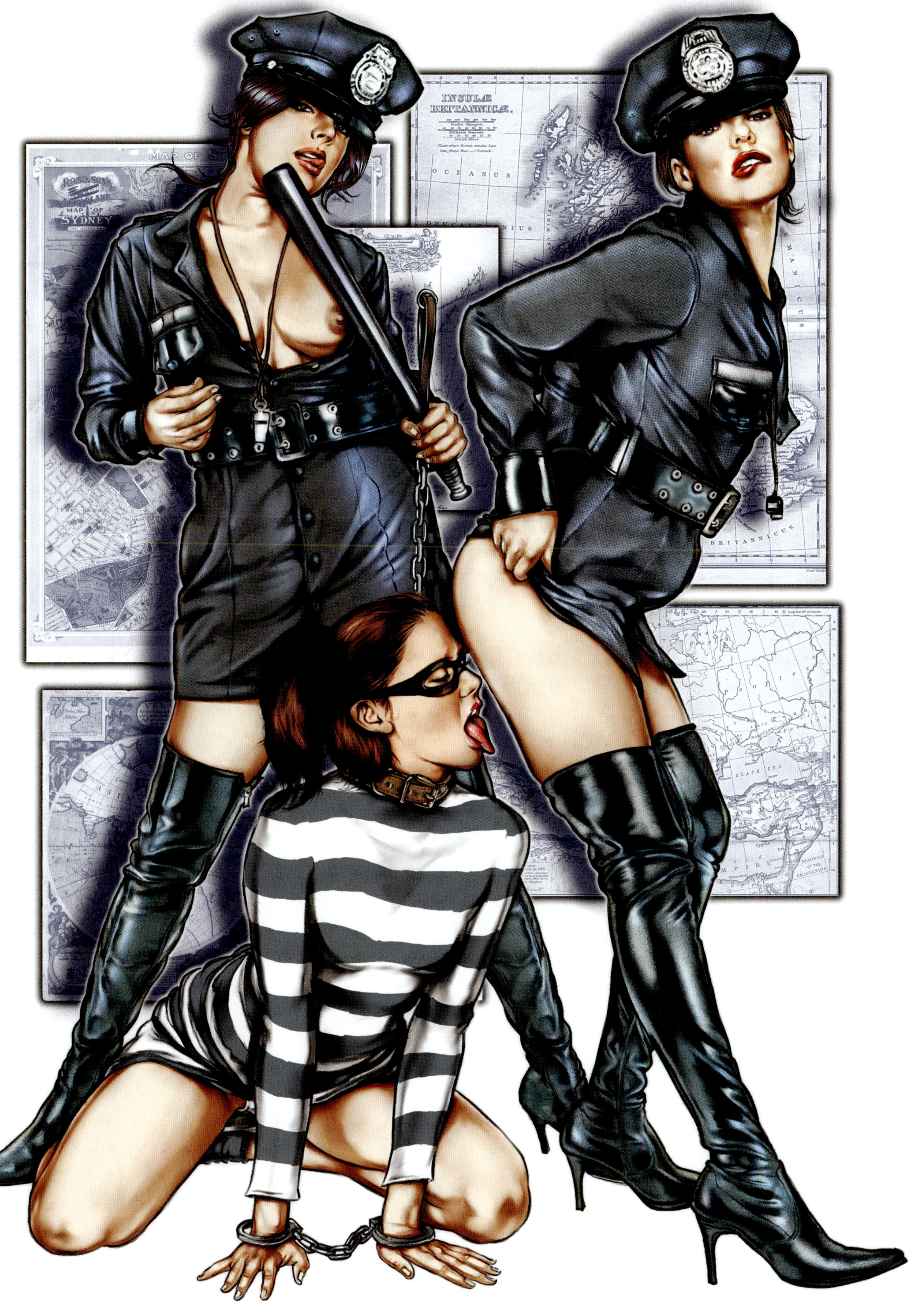
INSULÆ BRITANNICÆ.
OCEANUS
MAP OF SYDNEY
BRITANNICUS
BLACK SEA

The Punishment

A command from a teacher's assistant is *not* to be taken so lightly. She made it abundantly clear there would be no texting during the test. She found the two willful young girls who insisted on being so *very* disobedient, giving the TA no other choice but march them all into the janitor's closet and lock the door. Discipline must be maintained, or chaos will soon reign all over this private school. It's skirts up, panties down, paddle to the ready! Today's lesson will be learned. Harshly. Repeatedly. And with much enthusiasm!

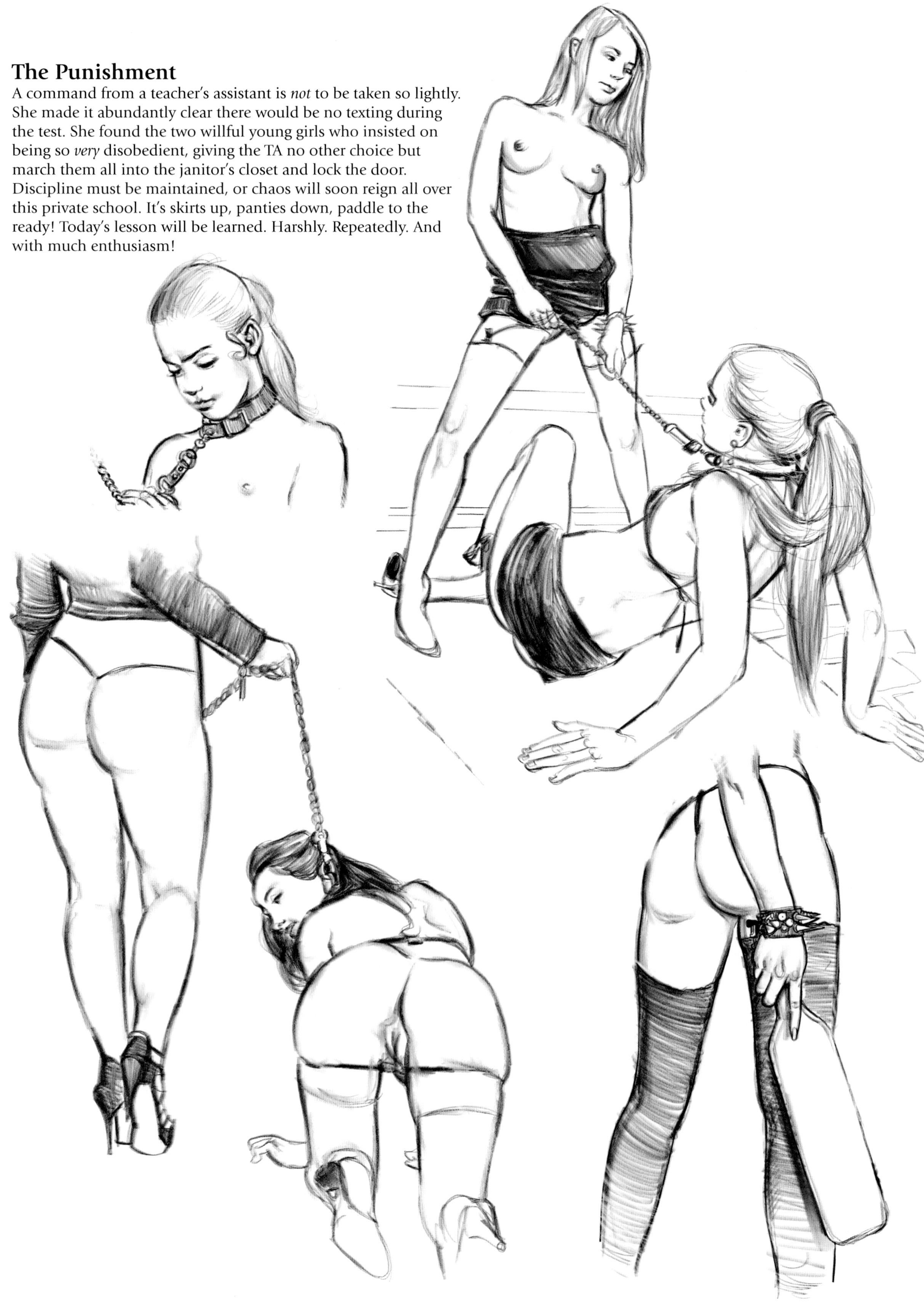

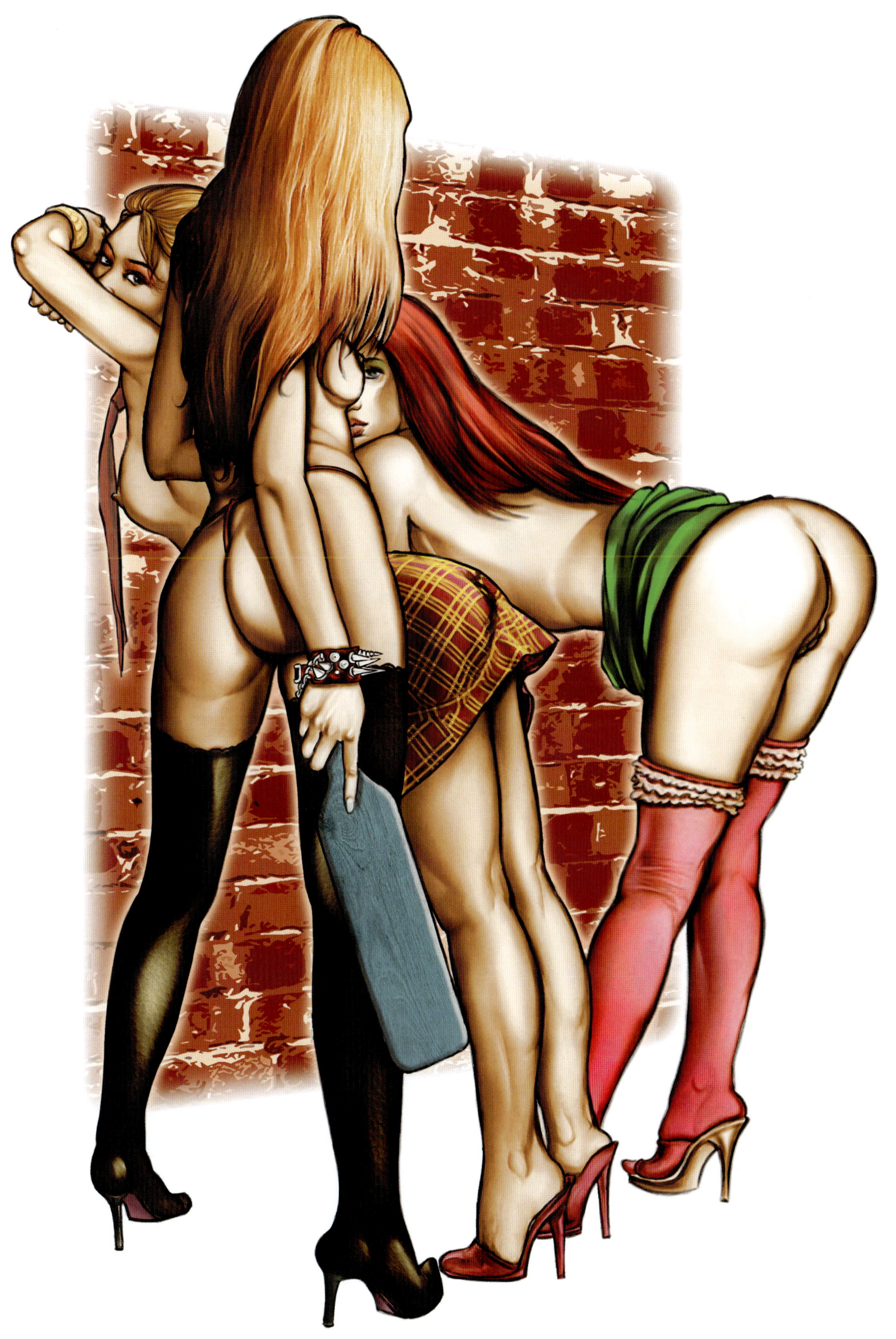

The Lady Loves Asses

She loves the firm round cheeks of a well-toned backside and wants them streaked crimson. Then bent forward to expose those glorious globes. Lashes sending waves of vibrating flesh that undulate under her practiced hand. Here finally is the wonderful signature of her work, etched in heat and bright red scratches against a field of virgin (near-virgin) white ass.

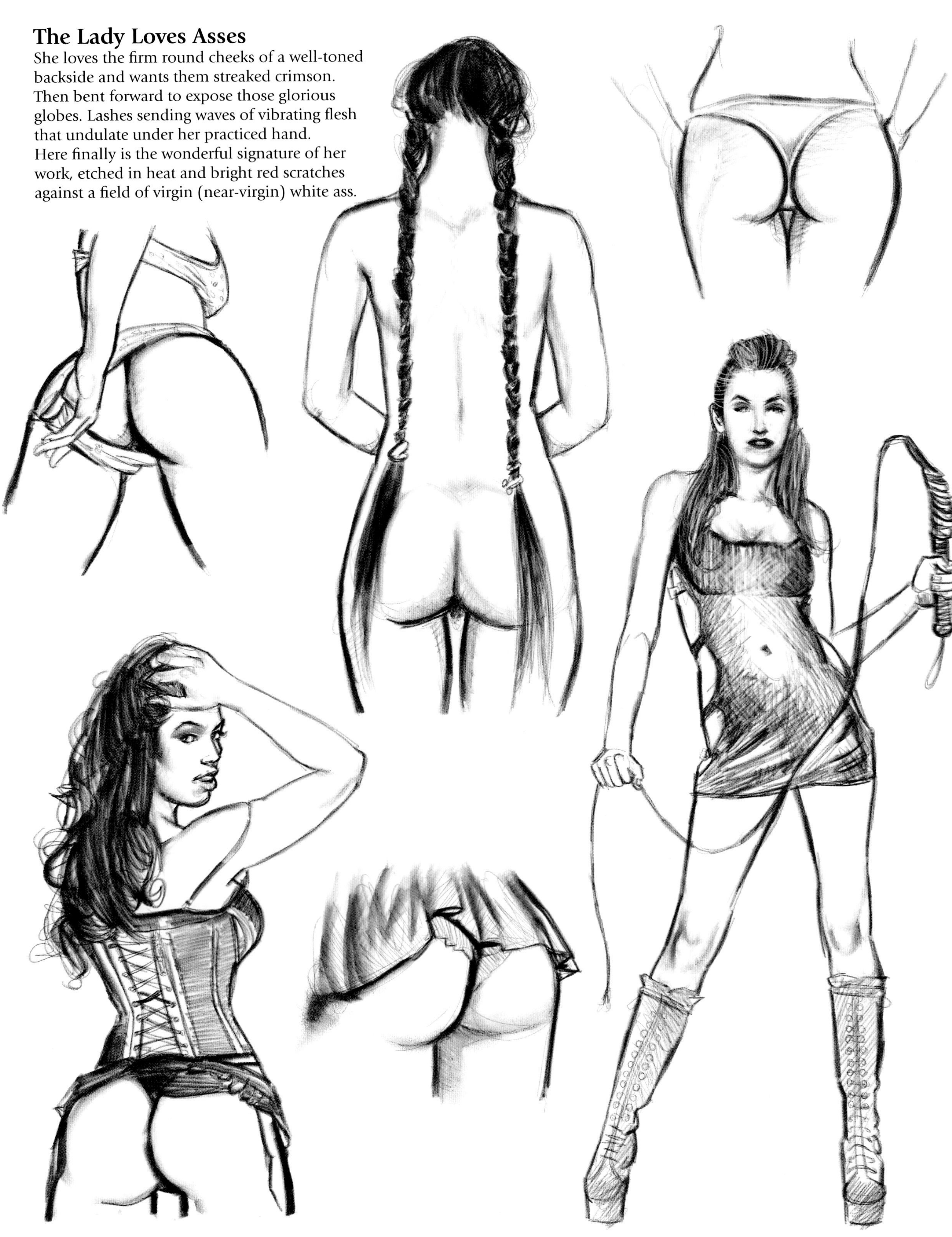

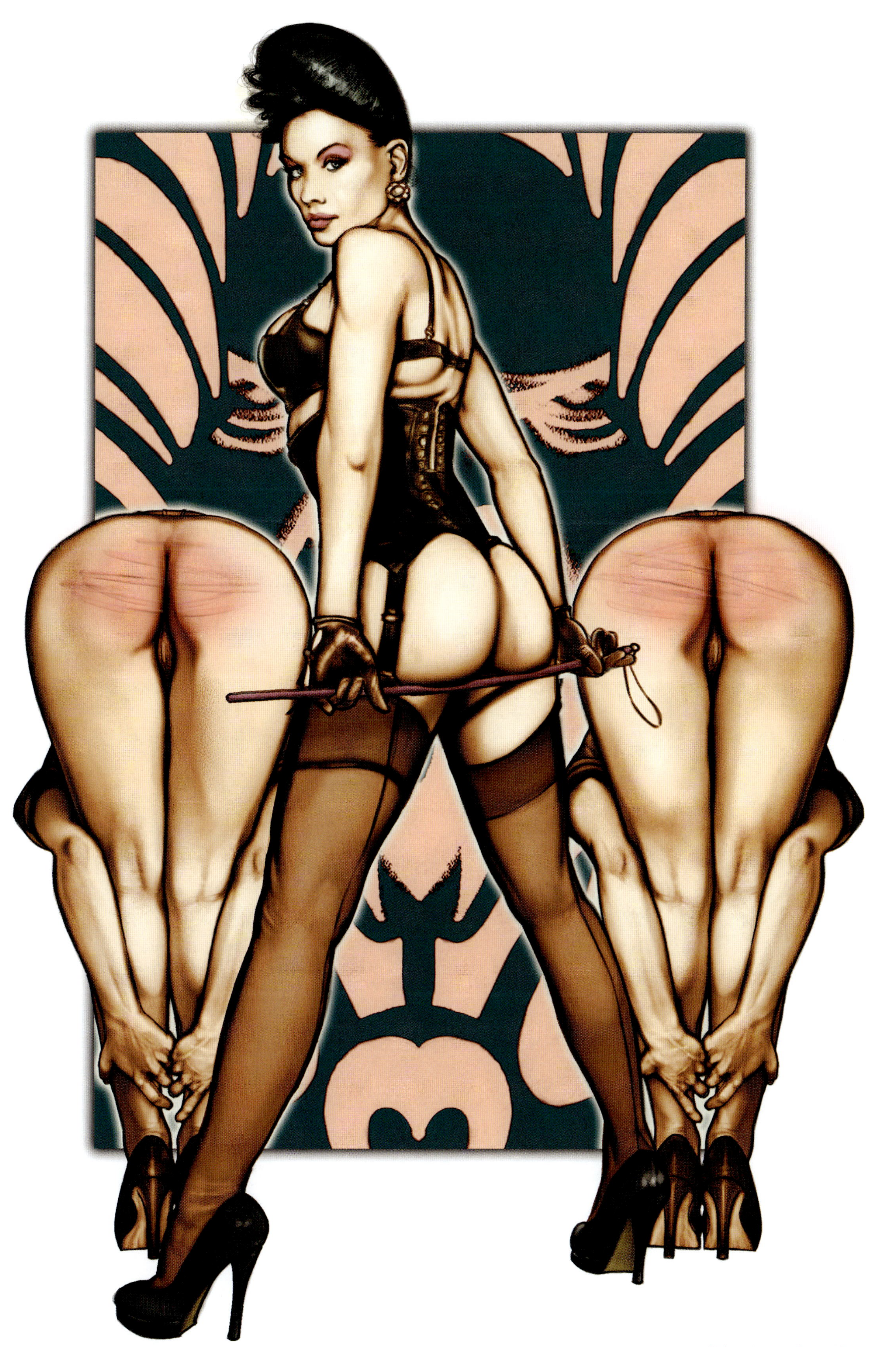

The Mistress' Maids

They've been working since they were 17, taking care of everything a mansion of this size requires. Learning on the job has made them clever, resourceful, and quick to please. This last trait has made them an invaluable resource for the lady of the house. While her husband is off on one of his many business meetings throughout the world, she's left alone to rattle about in a golden fortress. Ah, but help is just the ring of a tiny bell away. The mistress can summon her maids to the bedroom at any time to do some "light dusting" or serious redecorating. Whatever the mistress requires.

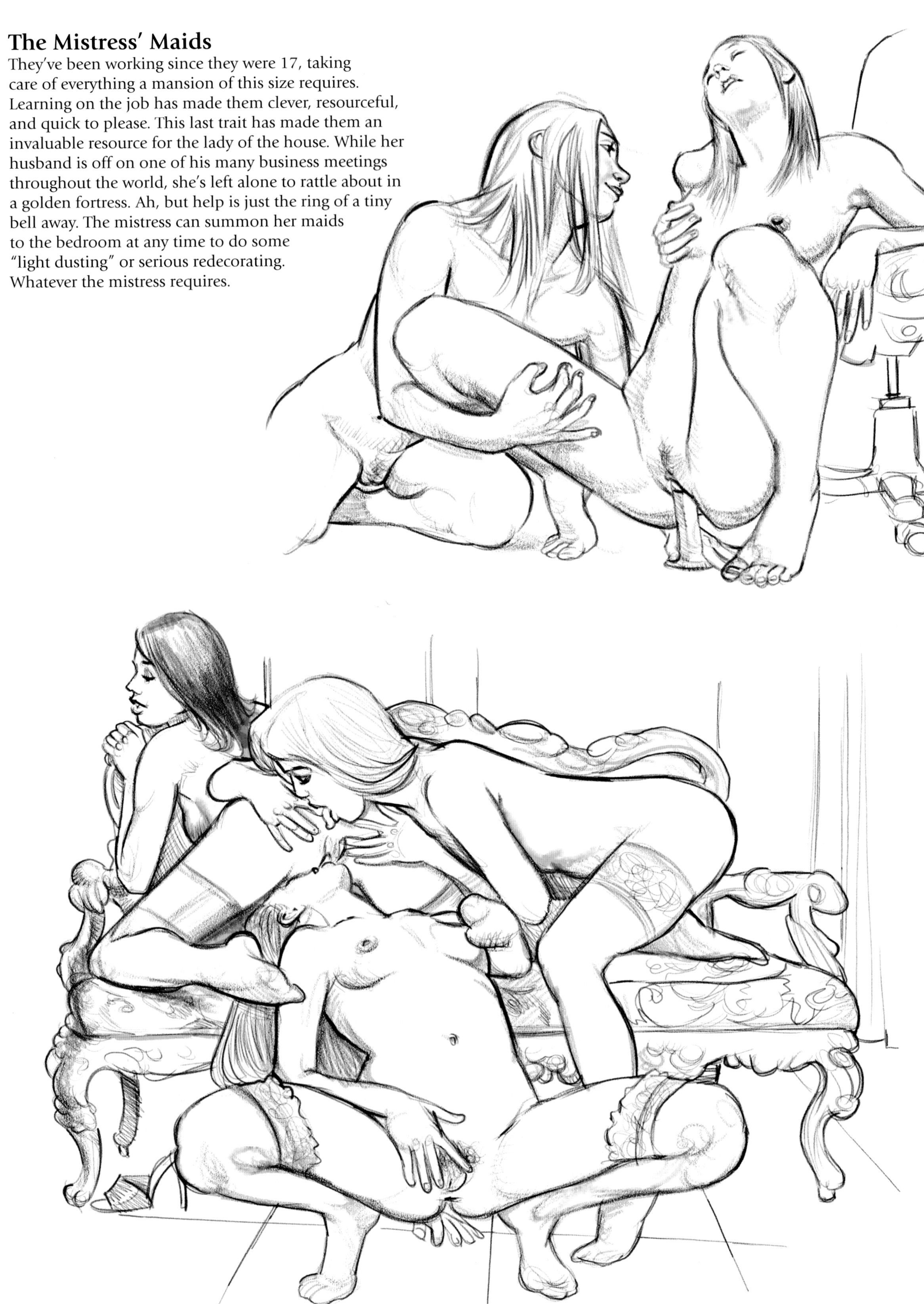

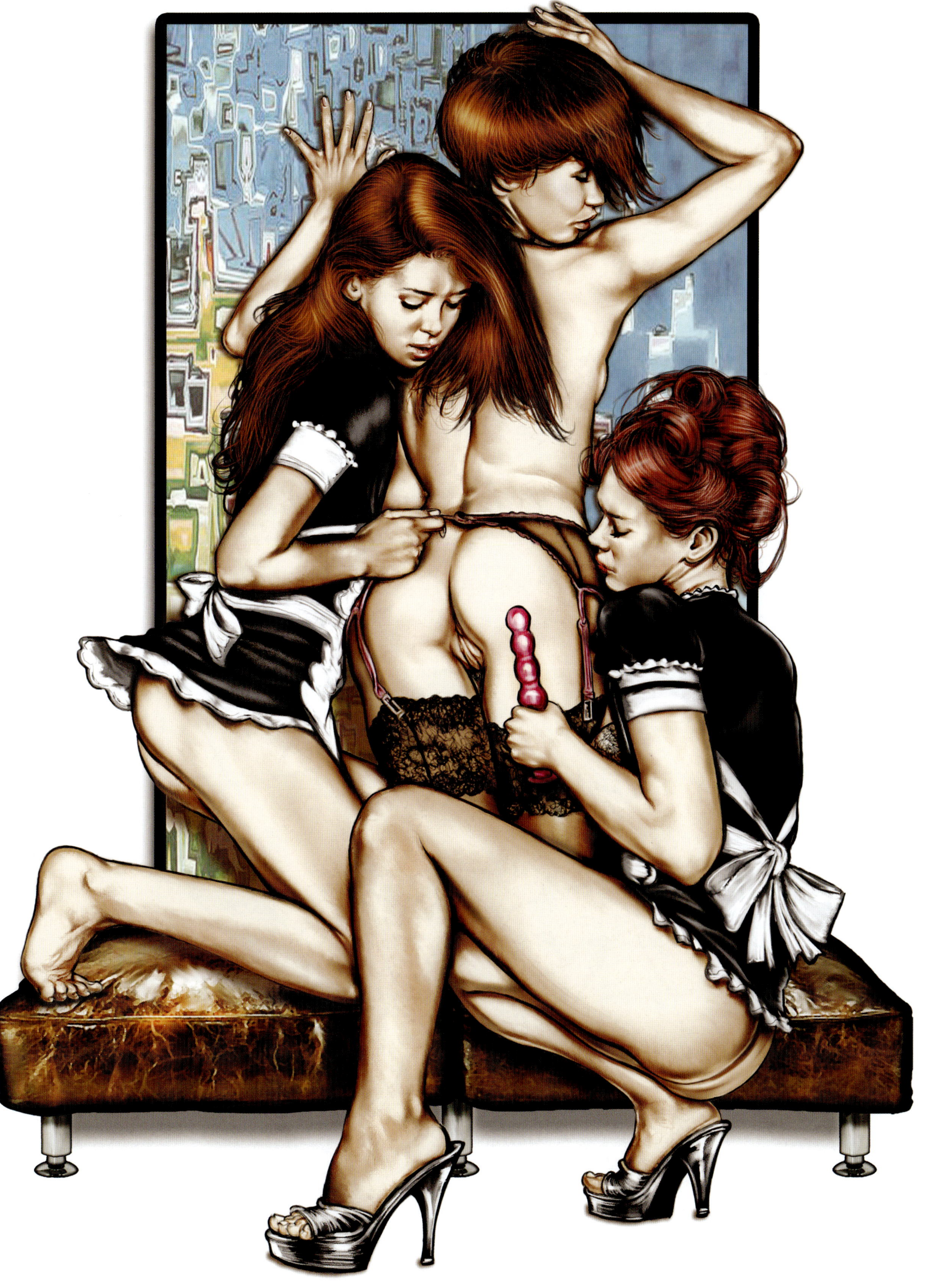

The Ladies Who Lunch

Always stylish, they can be found in the lazy afternoons of summer. They entertain with elegant manners in the elegant lounge. They've reached a level of success that comes with independence and intelligence. Men are nice, but not really necessary in their world. They flourish *in* their own company, *with* their own company.
Sophistication has its rewards.

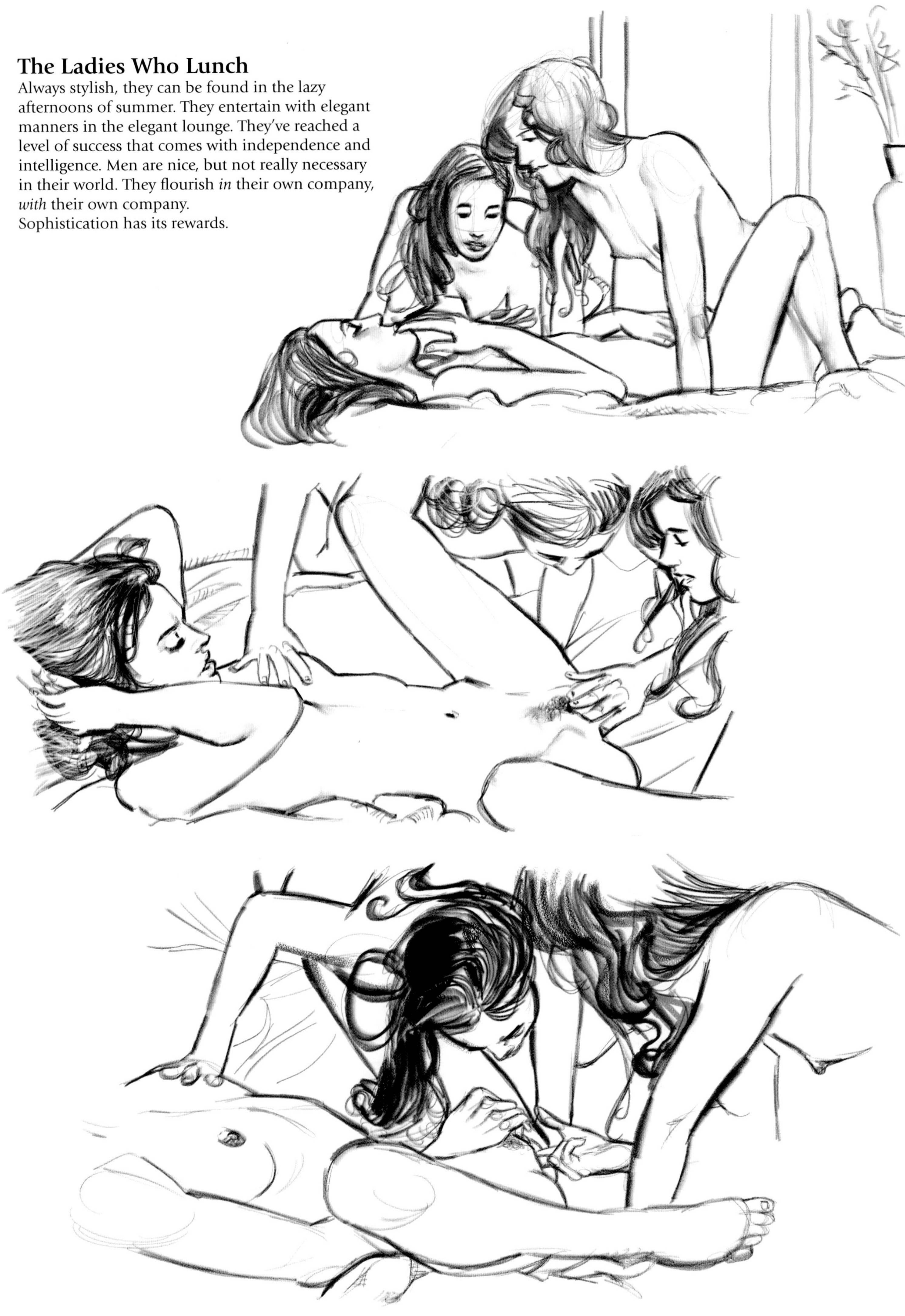

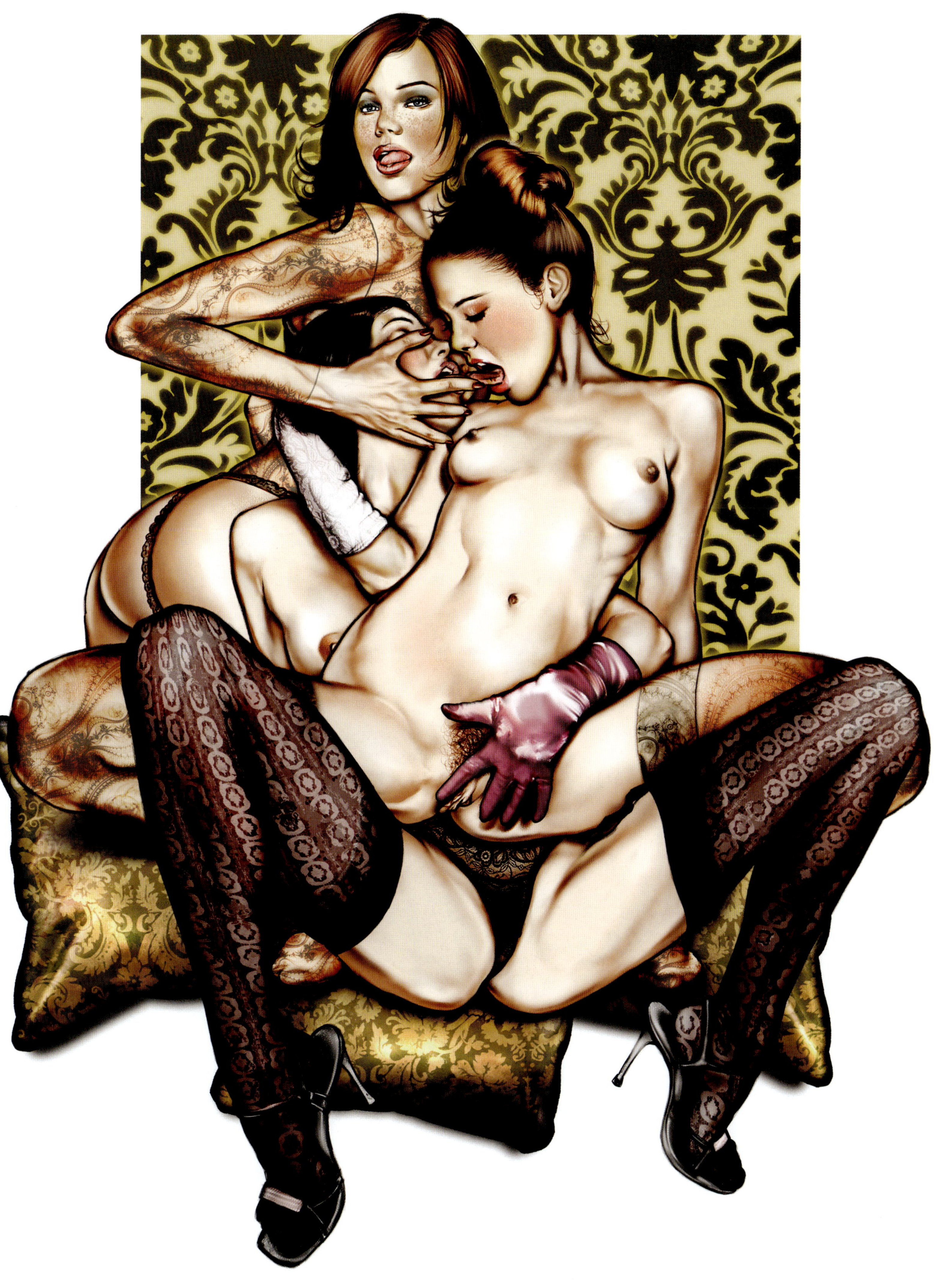

The Show

There are those who dabble in the lifestyle, and those who give themselves over completely to BDSM. The former think of it as adding a little spice with some slap and tickle. The latter know the exquisite joys that come with utter surrender of one's body and soul.
These ladies try to share that secret every Saturday night in a fully equipped dungeon in Los Angeles, near the airport. *"The Show"* accepts a pre-screened volunteer to experience the forbidden in a safe and loving environment. Every week, the list of volunteers gets longer!

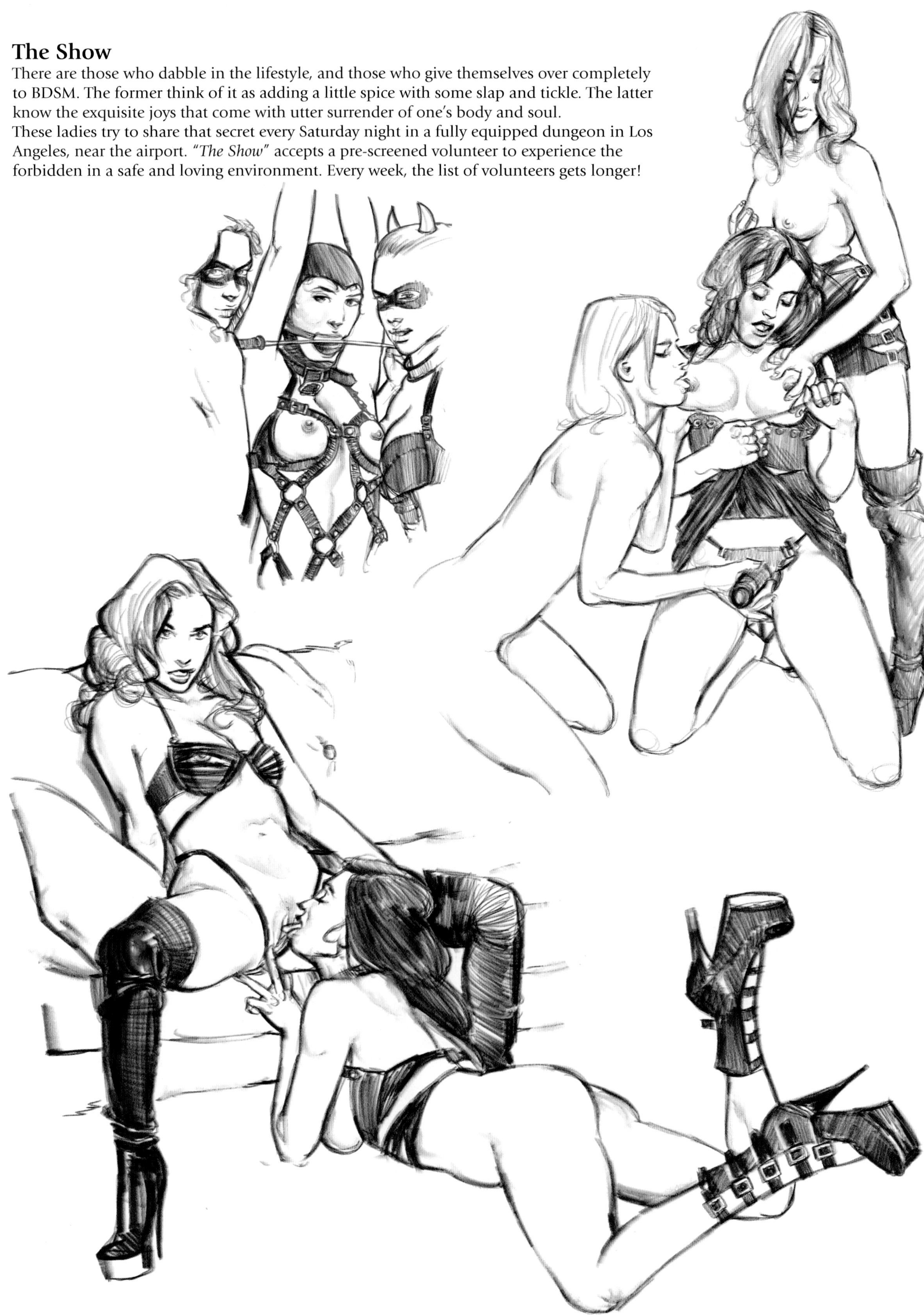

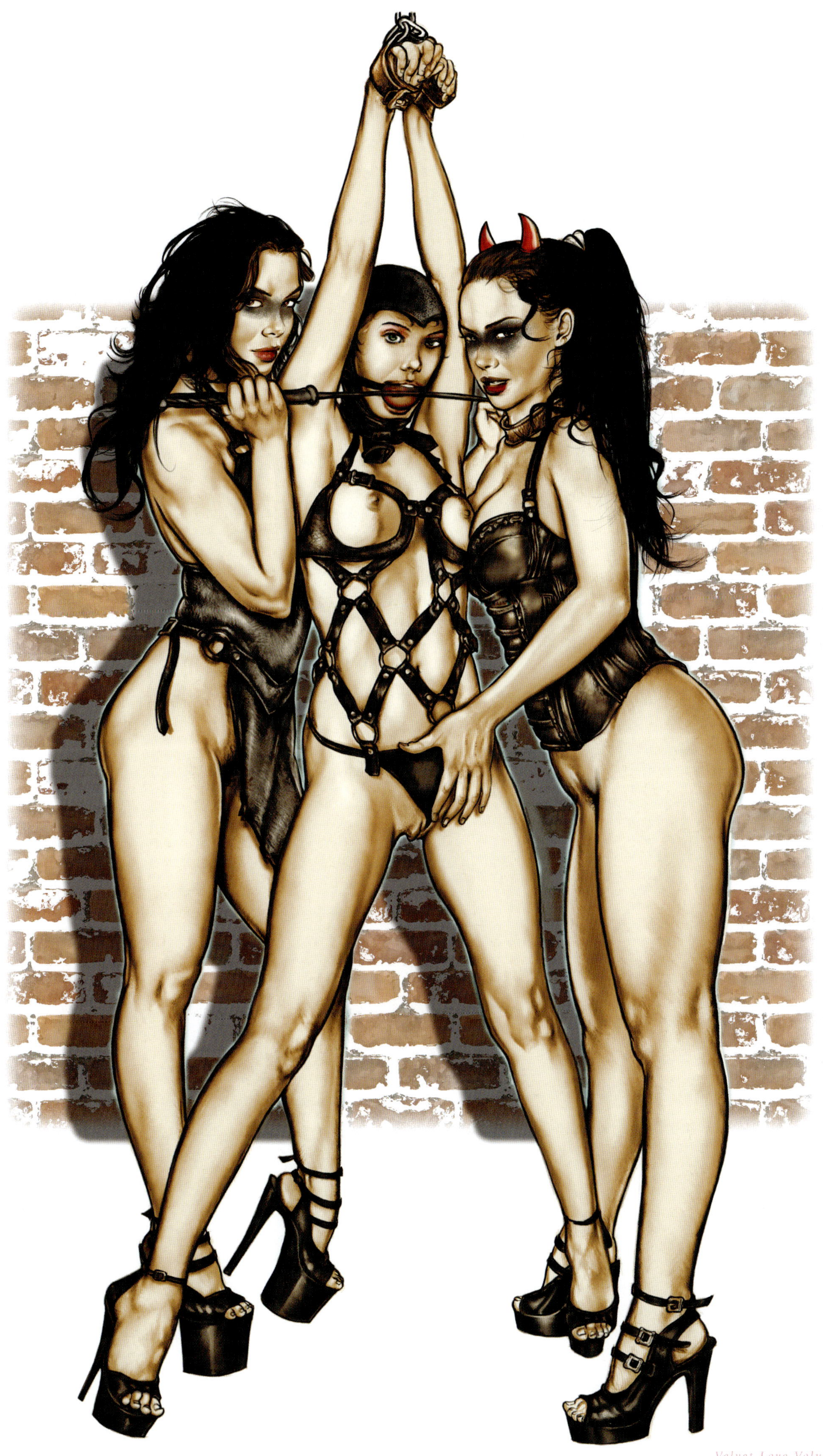

Driving

The race was long, taxing, dangerous. The noise, the speed, the split-second timing, it's all foreplay. A bet was made, a challenge was laid down and accepted. To the winner will come the spoils, and with so much power pulsing in their cars, so much raw, naked energy crackling in those engines ... well, there's foreplay and then there's *this* game! At the end, they've worked up such a an appetite for victory, who won is not the release they're interested in.
This is a winner's circle best enjoyed in private!

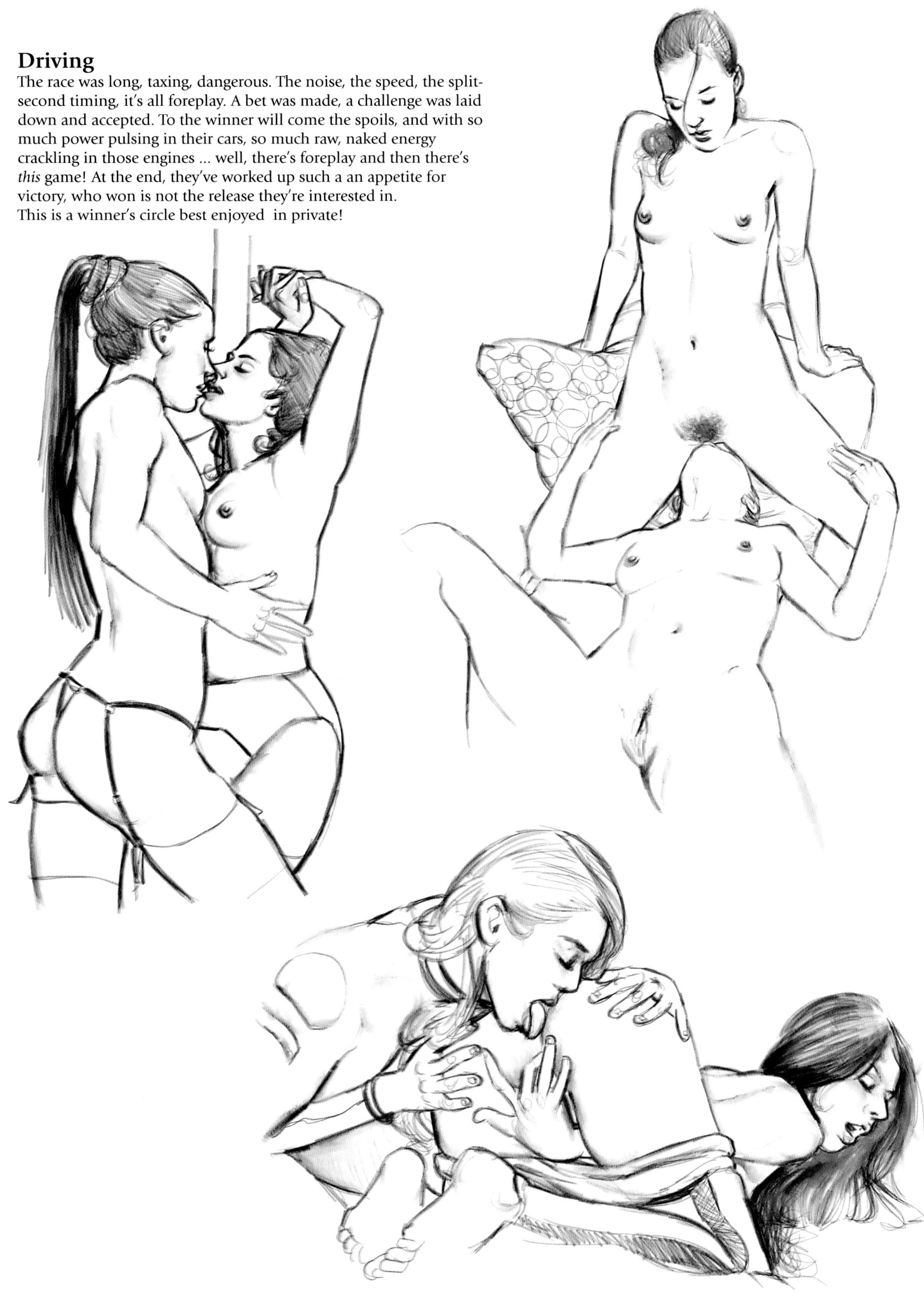

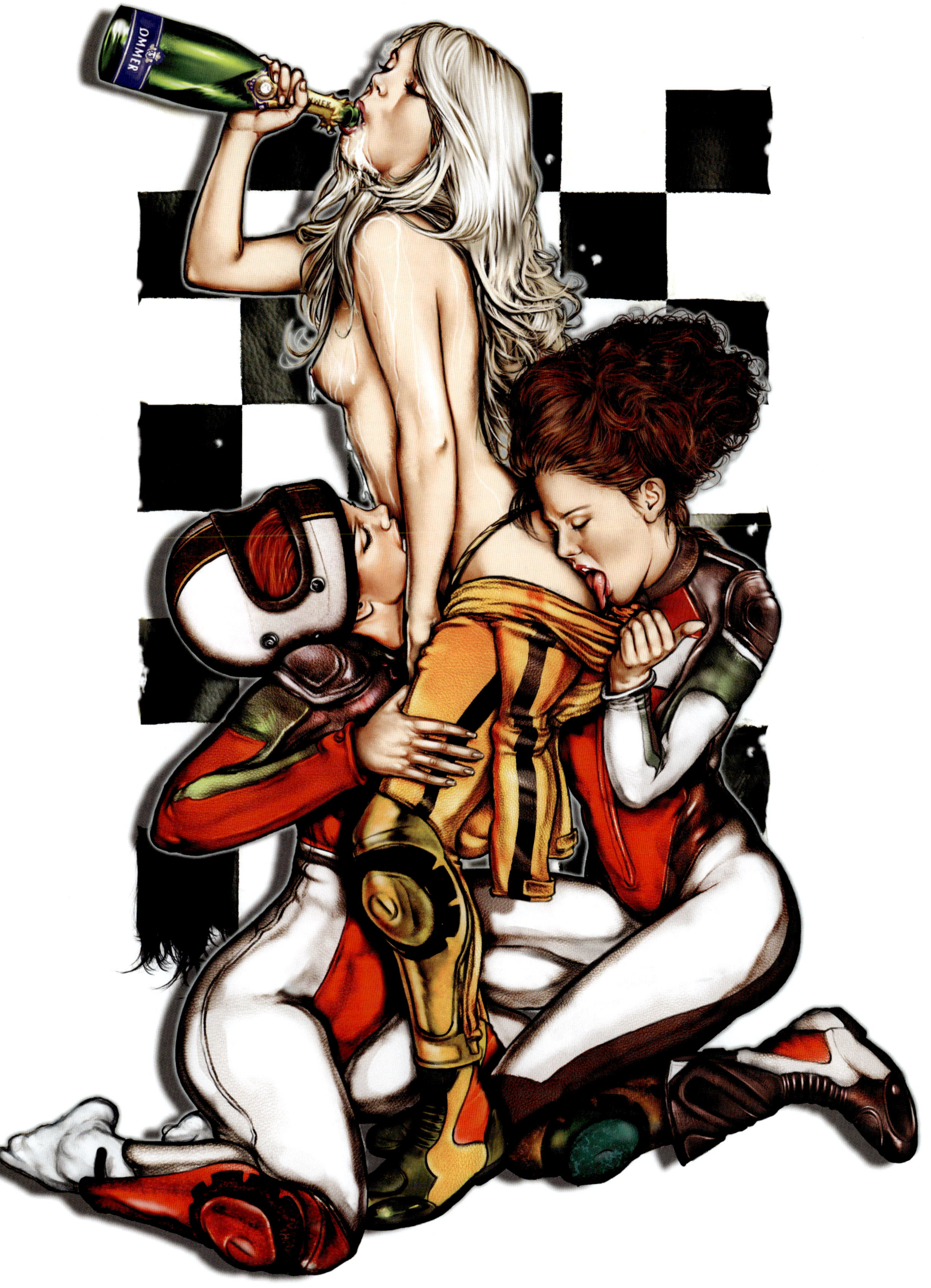

Passion for Fashion

The seamstress, a skilled crafts person who manufactures reality from designs created on paper. Such an intimate business. The customer stands to be measured. Hands taking necessary liberties to get proper fitting. Bare flesh brushing against sumptuous fabrics. Fingers pinching, caressing, working their skillful magic to make the client happy. So happy. What happens in the fitting room is a dark and glorious secret, and what emerges is a celebration of art and passion.
Mostly passion.

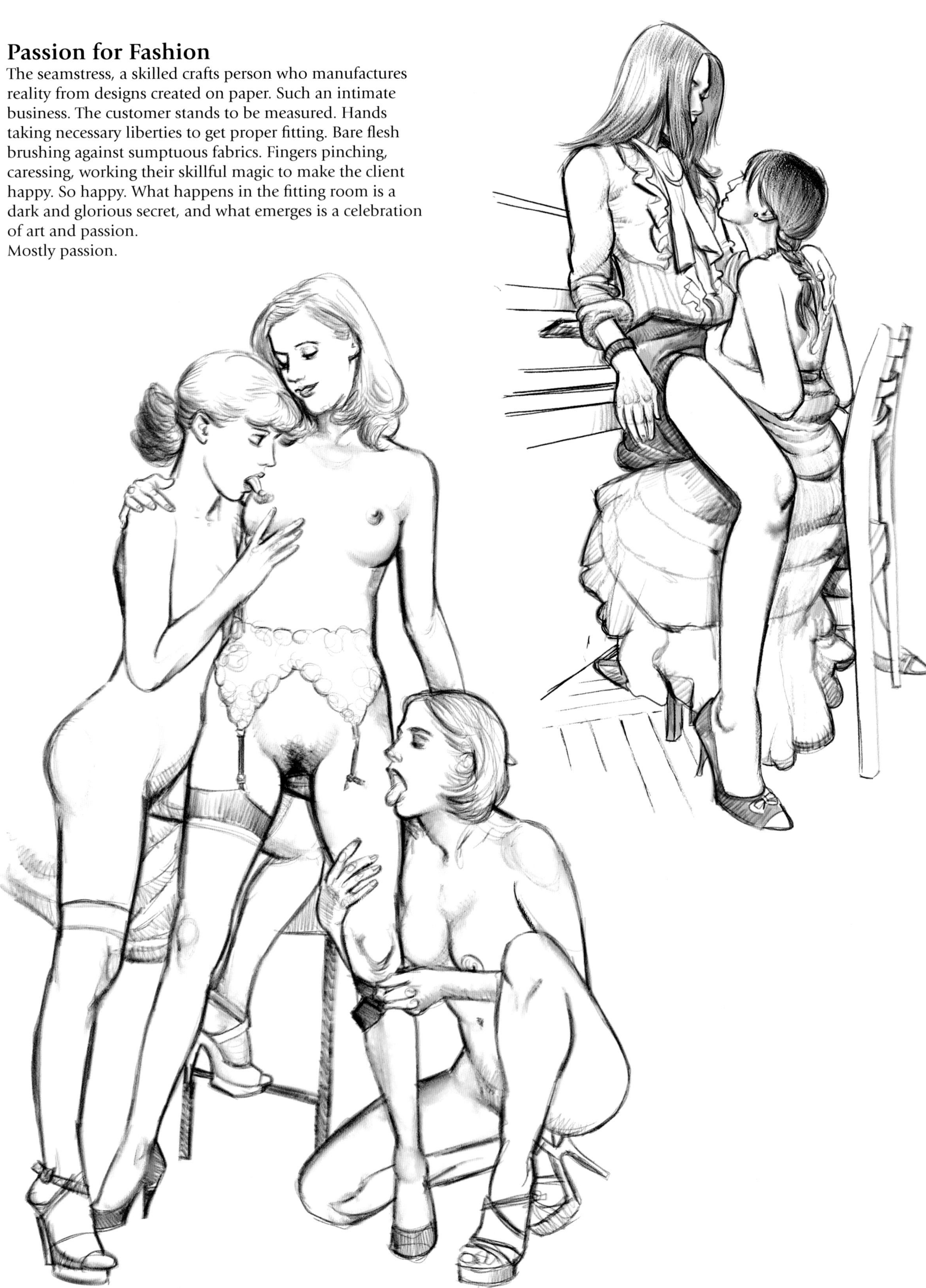

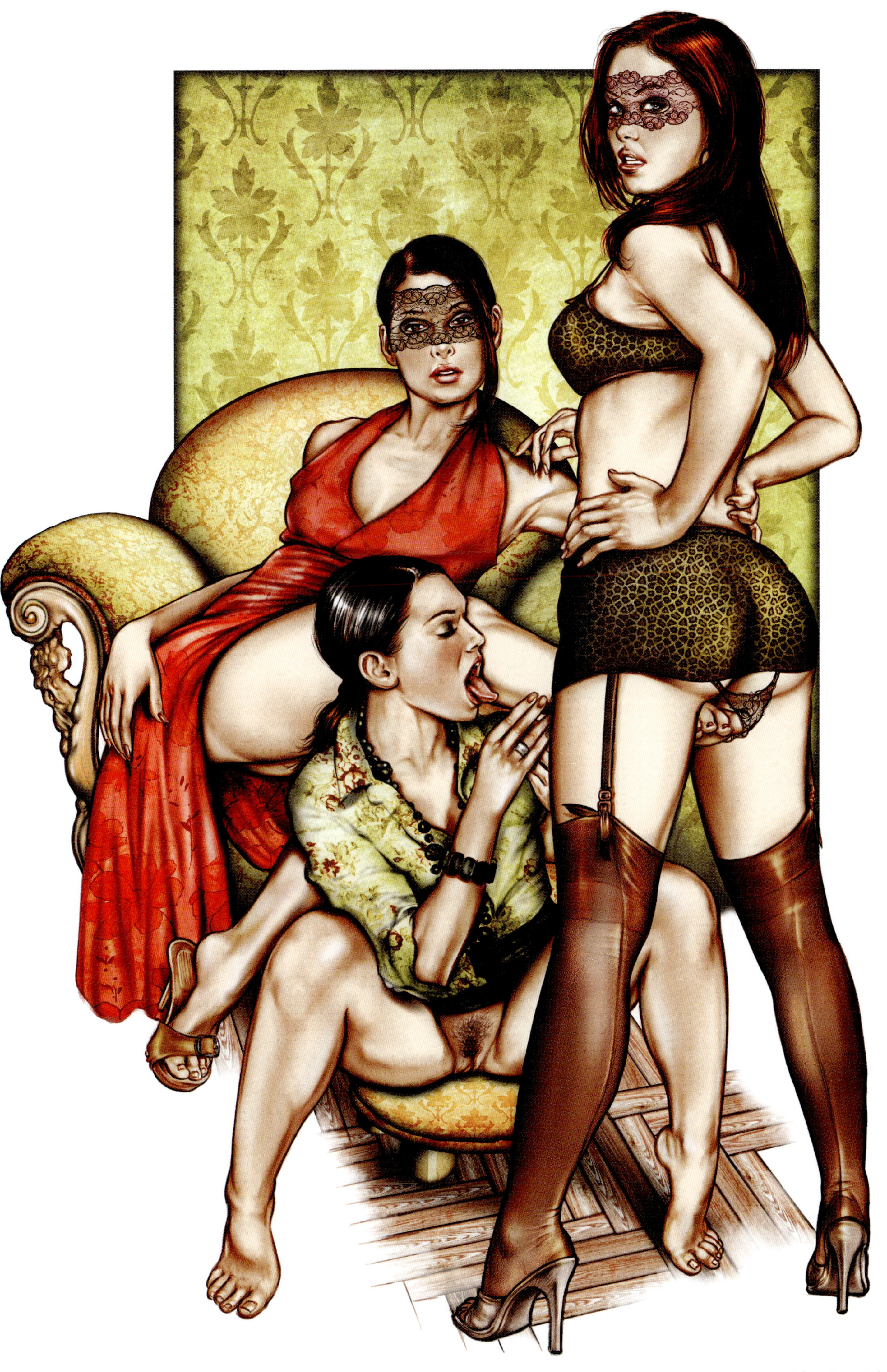

Silence

With words, lies can be made. Through language, falsehoods. Tonight, nothing will be said, but volumes will be understood. Everyone will be silenced, and only actions will speak. Bodies will touch, flesh will be tested, skin will sweat and strain against ropes cruelly tied. The sound of the moan and whimper will be permitted, but the cost will be dear. Tonight, we will see just how far we can go before the silence is broken by the cry *"no more!"*

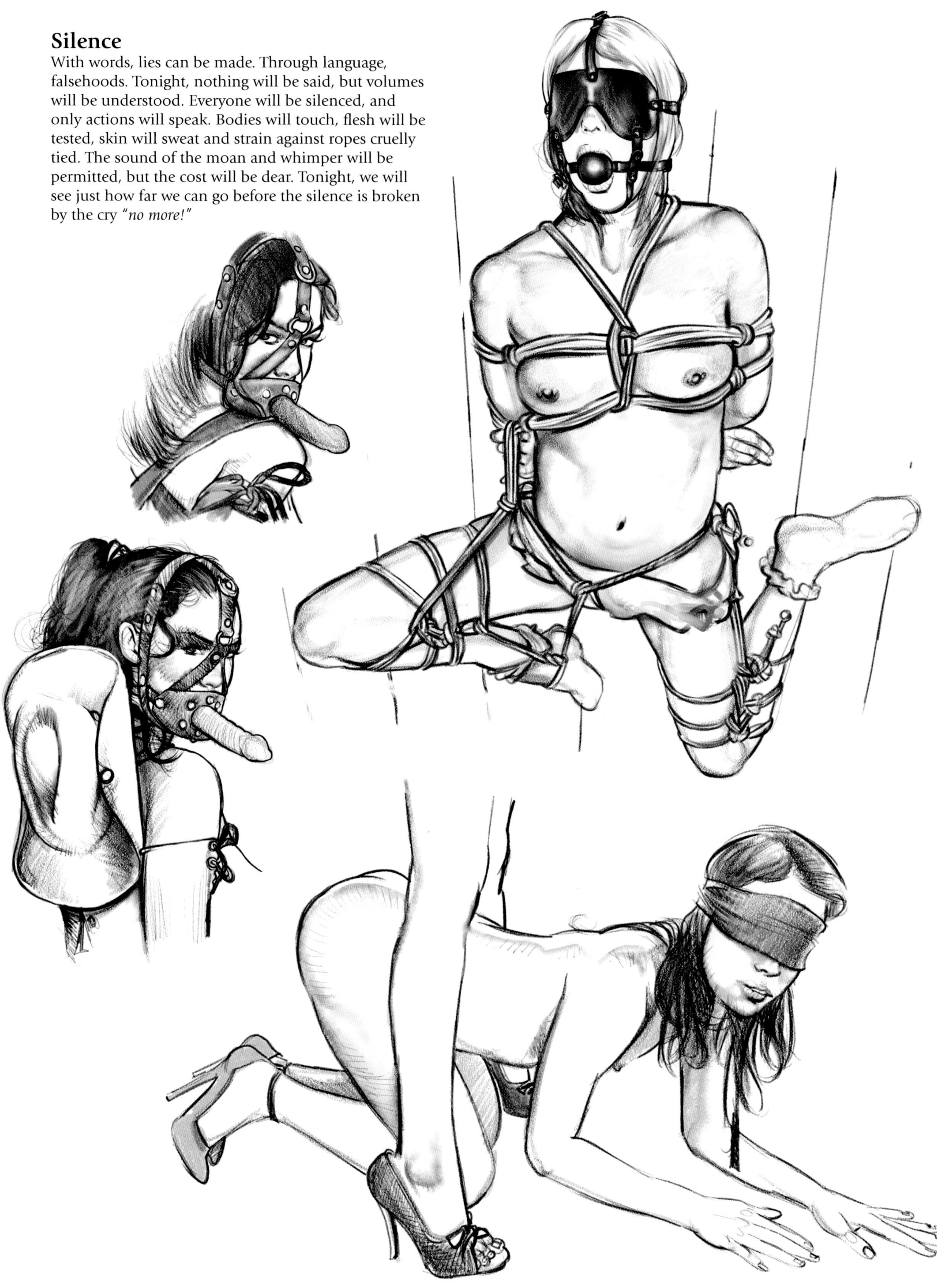

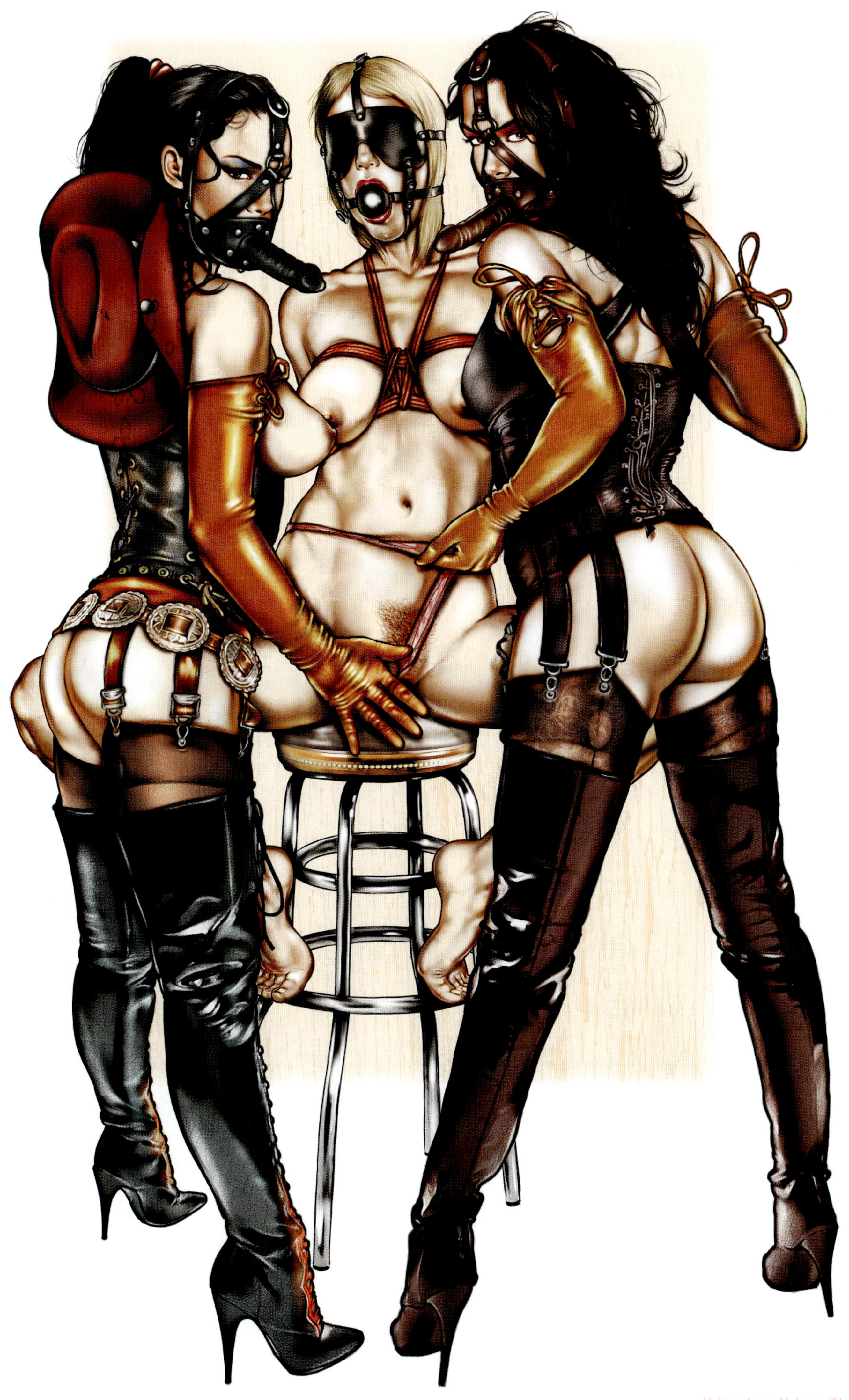

The Rule of Three

One, two and three ... All three "wrapped in a vortex of pleasure," as it was called in Nineteenth-century novels. All three, because in this book there are *always* three protagonists. Three is a perfect number - remember Pythagoras, a great lover of triangles, There is a supreme satisfaction in threes that humans are naturally attracted to.
Oh, but now there are four. Very well, let us celebrate the wonders of the quadrangle, the Four Horsemen...

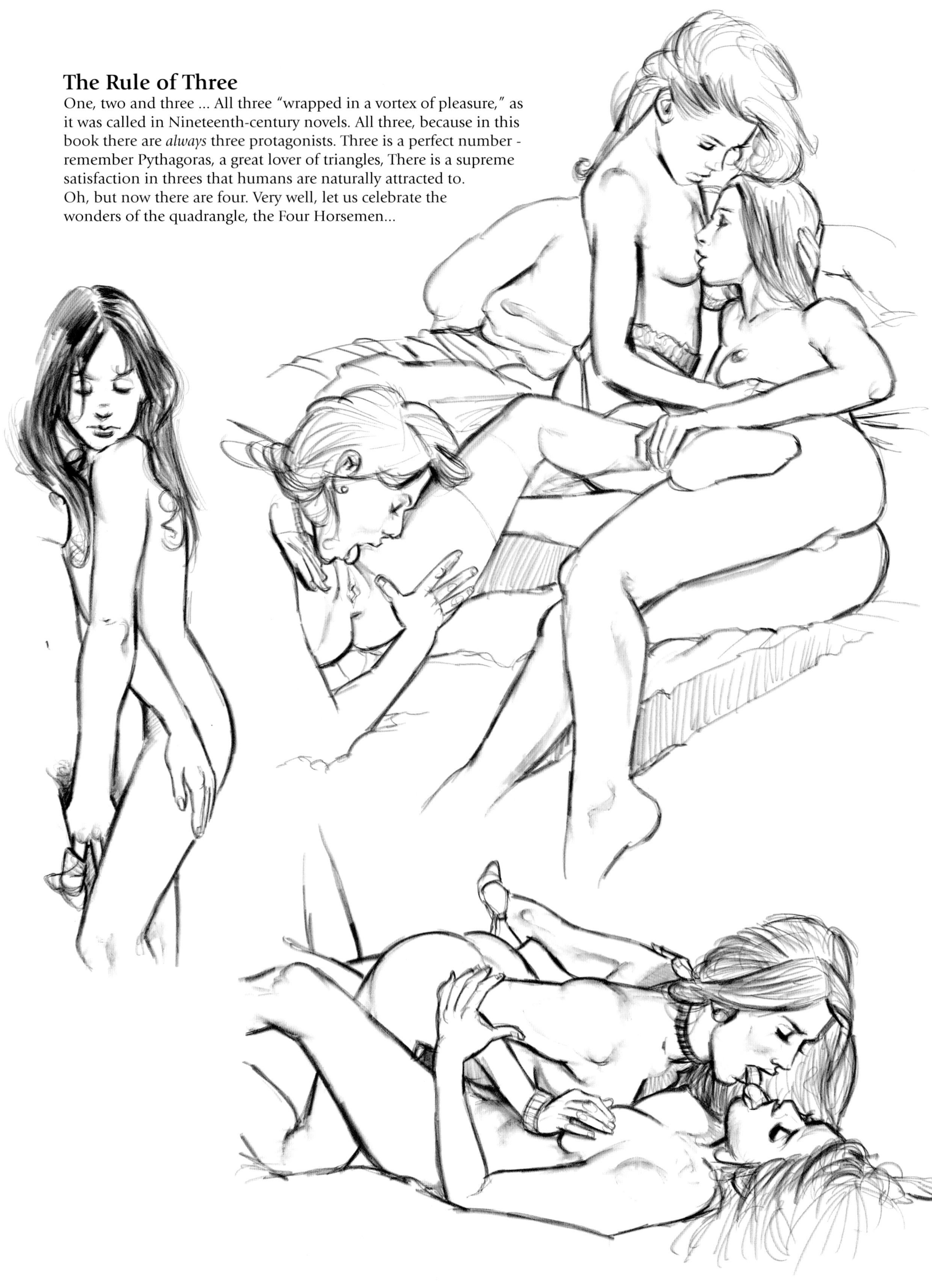

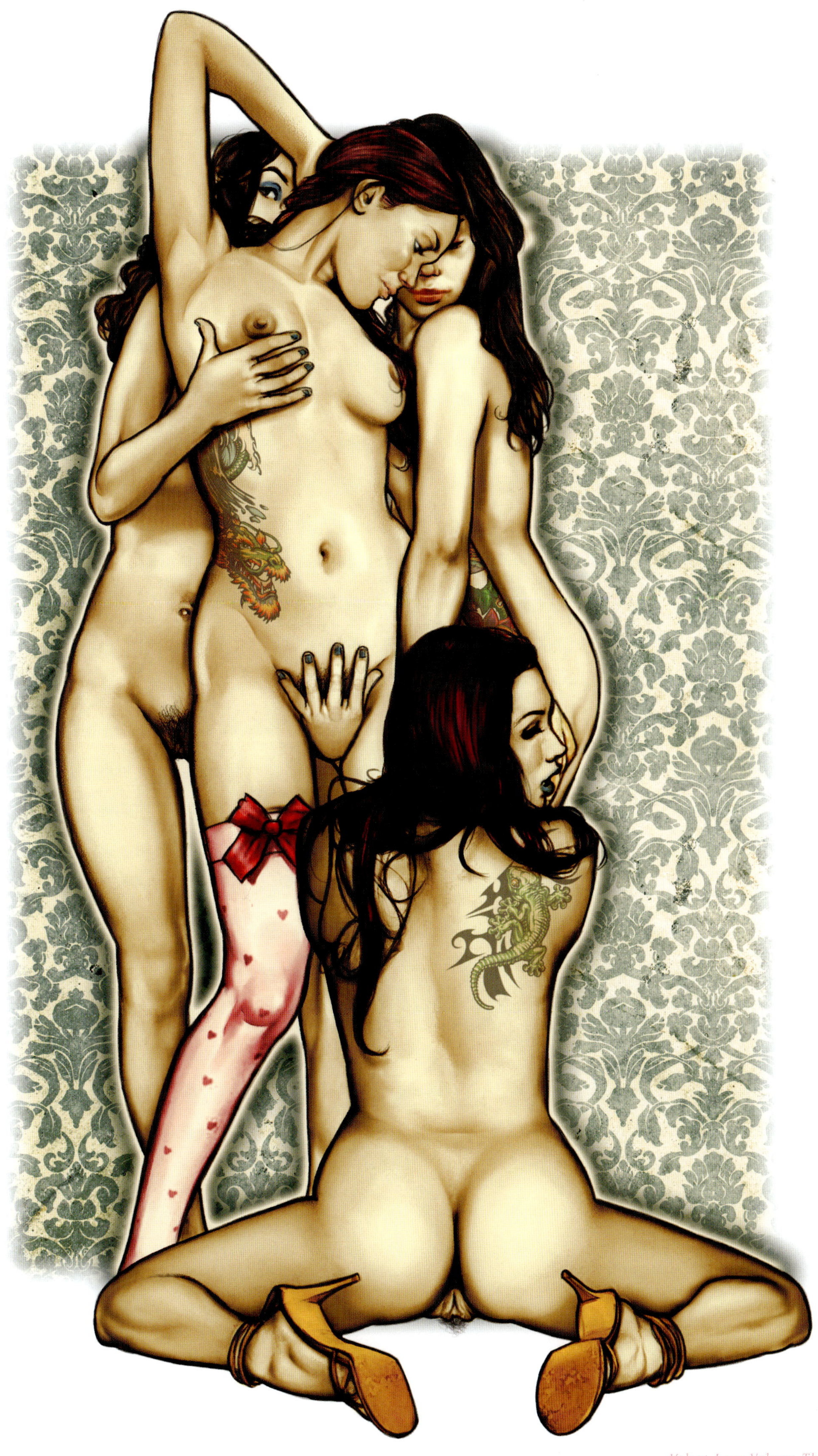

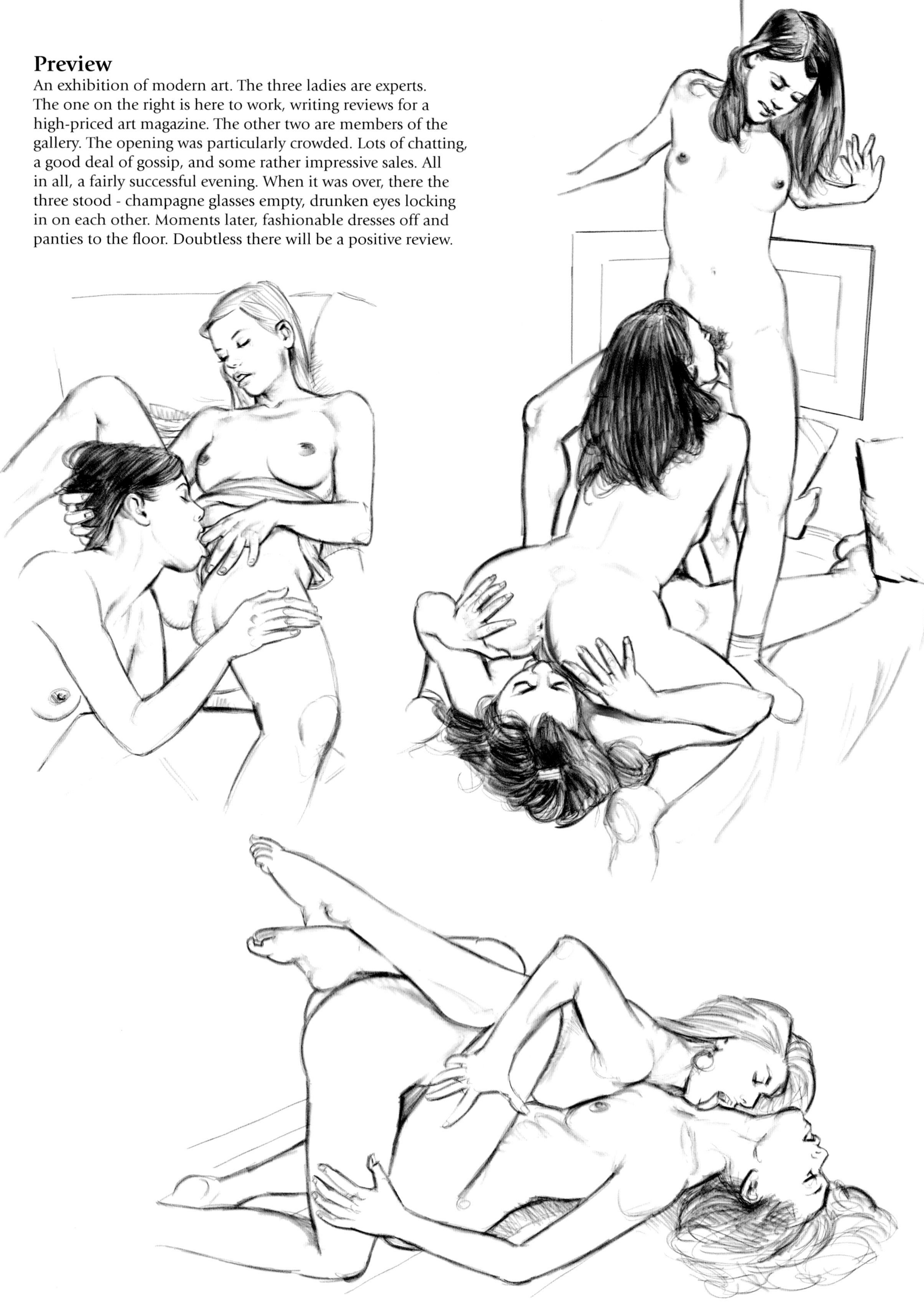

Preview

An exhibition of modern art. The three ladies are experts. The one on the right is here to work, writing reviews for a high-priced art magazine. The other two are members of the gallery. The opening was particularly crowded. Lots of chatting, a good deal of gossip, and some rather impressive sales. All in all, a fairly successful evening. When it was over, there the three stood - champagne glasses empty, drunken eyes locking in on each other. Moments later, fashionable dresses off and panties to the floor. Doubtless there will be a positive review.

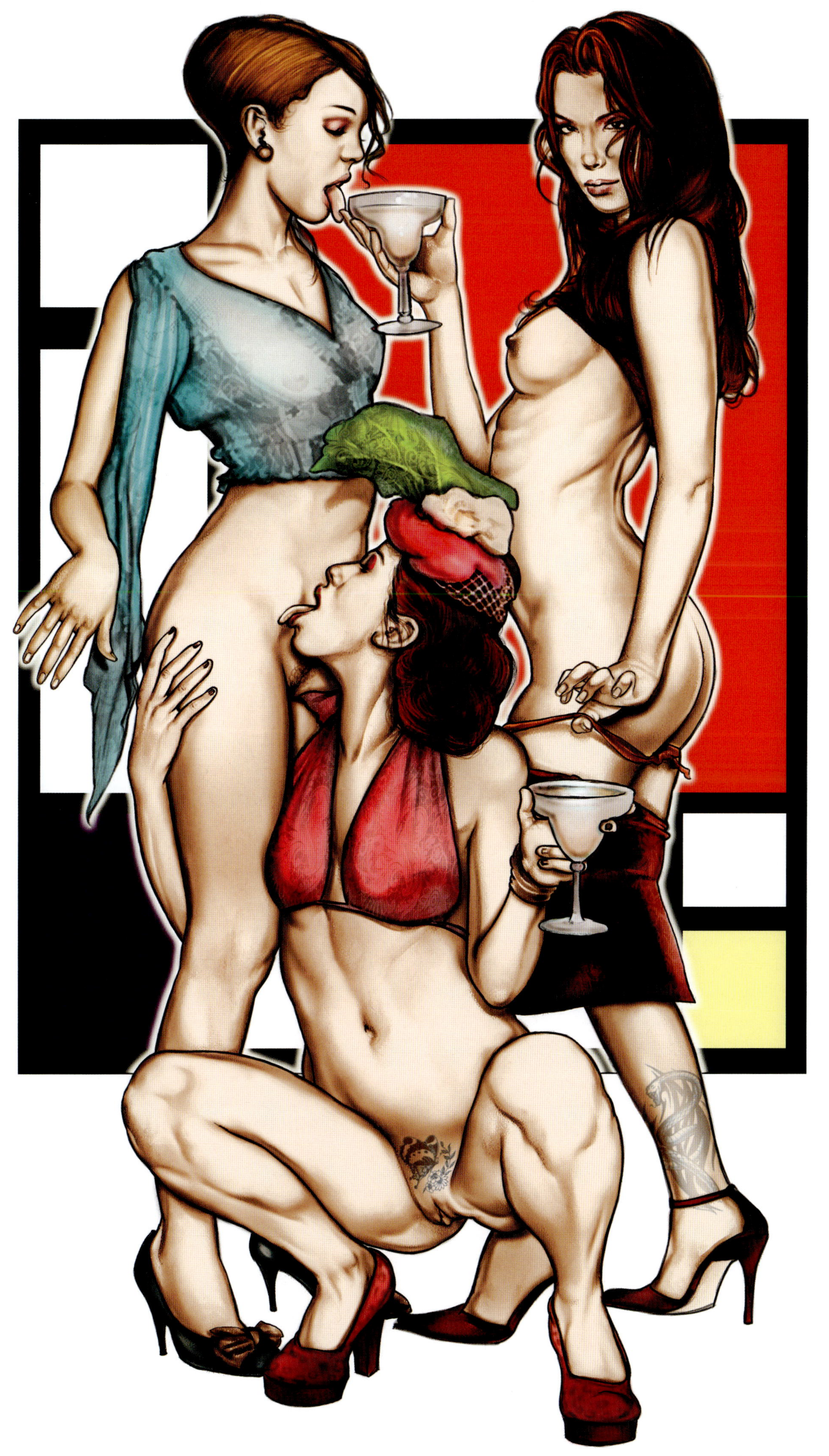

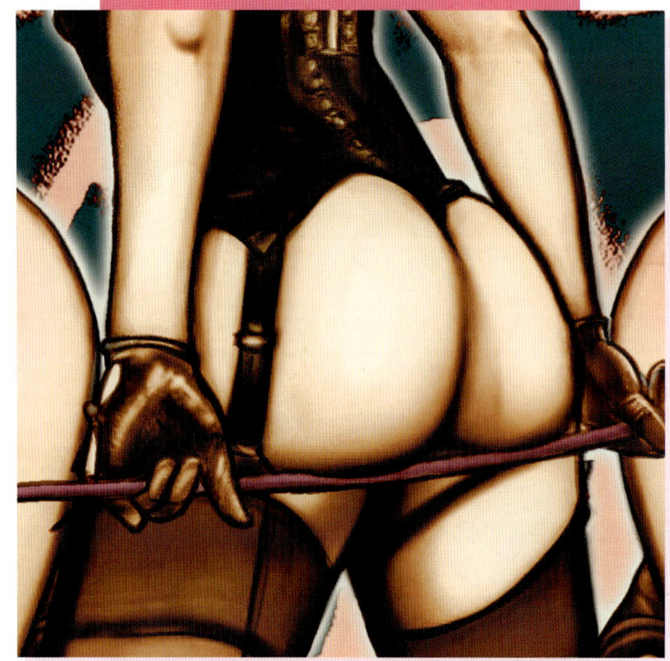

fin